VISIONS OF ROME

Thomas Ashby,
by Winifred Knights, c. 1922.
(Collection: Author)

VISIONS OF ROME:

THOMAS ASHBY, ARCHAEOLOGIST

by

RICHARD HODGES

The British School at Rome, London

2000

ISBN 0 904152 34 0

Cover illustrations —
Front: Drawing of Thomas Ashby by Winifred Knights c. *1922*
Back: Sketch by Winifred Knights c. *1921; Sketch by Giuseppe Lugli*
Cover design: Terry Wilkins

Typeset by Gill Clark
Printed by Stephen Austin and Sons Ltd, Hertford, Great Britain

**To Tommaso
&
Nicole**

England will still be England, an everlasting animal stretching into the future and the past, and like all living things, having the power to change out of recognition and yet remain the same

George Orwell, *The Lion and the Unicorn: Socialism and the English Genius*
(London, 1941), 70

CONTENTS

LIST OF FIGURES

PREFACE AND ACKNOWLEDGEMENTS

Every archaeologist, like every explorer and every hunter, has some
adventure to recount about his life in the countryside; fortunately,
archaeologists' adventures are almost always of modest purport and
have a happy ending.

Giuseppe Lugli, 'Piccole avventure romane di un archeologo militante',
Strenna di Romanisti 7 (1946), 42

The British School at Rome sits in a commanding position overlooking the
Valle Giulia, on the northern edge of the Borghese Gardens, in a wealthy suburb
of Rome. Its stark imperial façade bespeaks a grandeur that it has never, in
reality, possessed. Even when the School stood alone on a bald burnt hillside, it
was little more than a hollow shell, built in haste in the Indian Summer of the
British Empire. Yet, somehow, appearances count for much. If it ever possessed
one moment when its spirit equalled the ambition of Sir Edwin Lutyens's
design, it was under the direction of Thomas Ashby (1874–1931), Director of
the School between 1906 and 1925. Thomas Ashby junior, the School's first
scholar and third director, was a Wykehamist; graduate of Christ Church,
Oxford; Craven Fellow; topographer, archaeologist, art historian, bibliophile,
photographer and walker; a veteran of the First British Red Cross Ambulance
Unit on the North Italian front (1915–18); and, above all, a man of simple, 'late
Victorian', dignity.

Visitors to the School, of course, are seldom touched by Ashby's fate.
Their lot has tended to be a collegial time warp with the supreme opportunity to
tour Italy. Italy, so congenial to the visitor, in these cocooned circumstances is
little short of eternal paradise. But Italy has never been an easy country in which
to live. It takes much forbearance to come to terms with its whimsical oral
culture. Visitors, even those on nine-month scholarships, find this hard to credit.
More especially, such forbearance is beyond the imagination of those young
scholars turned academics or artists on their return to Britain, as it tends to be
beyond the imagination of any Briton. The gloom of dark moral judgement, like
the grey skies, tames the British; whereas, as Lawrence wrote, 'Italy does not
judge'.[1]

A certain sadness, then, stems from the fact that the School exists in a
timeless haven, but nevertheless seems invariably compelled to sustain the
indigenous moral judgements of its Anglo-Saxon councillors. This logic has
always been intolerably exacerbated by the cruel balance of funding. That the
School has survived without an endowment will not surprise anyone — the

British have always had limited respect for their culture, despite its profound qualities. As a race we forfeited our spirit to mercantilism. So it is some miracle that any British academic institute stands on foreign soil.

'Why has the British School at Rome survived', the then librarian asked me on my first day as Director in 1988? I ventured not to know, because she was going to tell me anyway. My eye was attracted to the dishevelled state of the Director's garden outside the window, ruinous for the want of a gardener, and the telling contrast with the shaded room lined with leather-bound books where we were sitting — once Ashby's sitting-room. The librarian's view was simple. The domestic staff kept the School going. It sailed on like a cruise-ship without a captain, despite the judgements sent from its tiers of well-meaning committees, despite the Directors sent from London, and despite the underfunding. But her homily was not altogether truthful. The ship steered a course navigated by its illustrious founders. She knew all too well that in this curious limbo there were the ghosts of Thomas Ashby and his long-standing Assistant Director, Eugénie Strong, who had established the spirit of the place.

Ghosts — I exaggerate! Eugénie Strong, I believe, does haunt the place, especially the library. She appears only to men. She remains, I surmise, because she bitterly regrets the cataclysm she caused before she left the School in 1925. Ashby's ghost, by contrast, has never been seen. His spirit, at least, sleeps soundly. It is those who have followed him who have not. Hence, metaphorically speaking, his ghost does haunt the place. We are awed by his achievement.

Listening to the librarian in 1988 I sensed that the history of the School could only be truly grasped if the story of Ashby was told — 'exorcized'. I was mystified by the institutional judgement that he was a poor administrator, an old-fashioned scholar, and a bluff and distant person. Much of this is gleaned from Peter Wiseman's thoughtful history of the British School at Rome.[2] Wiseman fashioned a characteristically absorbing study, lending pride of place to Ashby's era. But he acknowledged that his essay amounted to no more than a sketch. A detailed biography, in fact, is impossible, given the absence of adequate documentary materials. Ashby's diaries and most of his letters have long since disappeared, although the British School does house a miscellany of documents, notebooks and papers bequeathed to it by May Ashby after her husband's death. Only his voluminous photographic albums (and 9,000 negatives, in the Gabinetto Fotografico of the Istituto Centrale per il Catalogo e la Documentazione, Rome) survive, serving as diaries of a kind. The albums themselves are kept in the archive of the British School. As to other sources, those who met him, if they survive, are in their late eighties or nineties. Therefore I have had to draw upon the School's administrative records, including the letters of Ashby and Eugénie Strong to the School's London-based Secretary, Evelyn (later Sir Evelyn) Shaw. I have also used the School's Annual Reports to furnish a chronology for much of Ashby's activities. However, as there is no detailed catalogue of these documents,

I have chosen to refer often to Wiseman's volume to facilitate, wherever possible, access to the sources.

Unearthing Ashby has been by no means straightforward. As a result, I have set out to fulfil a more modest objective. Ever conscious of my introductory conversation with the librarian, I felt that it was important to set the record straight about Ashby as a person, and then to tell, as fully as possible, the story of his life as an academic, as the Director responsible for building the British School at Rome in the Valle Giulia, as an ambulance-driver in the First World War, and as the victim of the British tendency towards dark moral judgement, to which Lawrence referred.

It is not difficult to discern that this is a Director's portrait of a Director. It is a commentary upon meeting the twin challenges of creativity and leadership in administration. In writing it I should like to express my special thanks to Professor Peter Wiseman, who has been unstintingly encouraging and helpful; someone whom I feel certain would have found it easy and rewarding to have collaborated with Ashby. My warmest thanks, too, to Alistair Crawford and Karin Einaudi, who kindly read and commented upon a draft. I should also like to express my debt to the following, who in one way or another helped with this project: Bruno Bonelli, George Boon, Richard Brewer, David Cannadine, Amanda Claridge, Gill Clark, David Colvin, Joseph Connors, Lucos Cozza, Philip Freeman, Michael Fulford, Oliver Gilkes, Colin Hardie, Robert Jackson, the late Richard Krautheimer, John Mitchell, Nicoletta Momigliano, Oswyn Murray, Cassy Payne, Margaret Poulter, the late Ralegh Radford, Colin Renfrew, Ruth Rubinstein and Rita Turchetti. I owe a special debt to my research assistants, who sifted through the School's archives: James Murdoch, George Anelay and Tom Stuttard. My warmest thanks also to Sally Martin, my ebullient and energetic personal assistant in 1993–5. Valerie Scott, the School's Librarian, has been selflessly helpful. I am very grateful to Gill Clark for her thoughtful and exacting editing of the text. Finally, I should like to record my debt to my long-suffering children, Charlotte and William, who shared my seven years in the British School, to Maria Pia Malvezzi Campeggi, to Tommaso and Filomena Astolfi, whose friendship and kindness has been beyond gratitude, and to Nicole Coolidge Rousmaniere for her wonderful support and encouragement.

April 2000

1

Quel Caro Ashby

I knew that even in going to the abode of the
dead he was not going without the protection of the
Gods, and that when he arrived there it would be
well with him if ever it was well with any one …
So that it was not for him that I wept: I wept for
myself, in losing such a friend.

Phaedo, 58e, 117e [1]

Thomas Ashby disembarked in Southampton on the morning of Friday 15 May
1931. He had taken the roundabout voyage back to Britain from Italy. Perhaps his
trips to America and Australia had given him a liking for sea voyages. The
purpose of his visit was particularly British. His old college, Christ Church,
Oxford, had decided to appoint a restricted number of Senior Research Students.
Ashby was the first and only one appointed in 1930. A condition was attached.
Thirty days' residence was required every year. Ashby had come to satisfy the
regulation. He boarded a first-class carriage on the 9 a.m. express for
Waterloo.[2] Between New Malden and Raynes Park, twenty minutes or so from
Waterloo, he tumbled from the train and died. The guard of the train testified to
the coroner that the carriage door could only have been opened from the outside,
by lowering the window. A local doctor testified that the post-mortem
examination revealed a tumour lying against the right-hand lobe of the
cerebellum, which must have caused him pain and giddiness. This, the doctor
believed, accounted for the numerous pairs of glasses found on Ashby's body. A
letter to his wife was also found amongst his belongings, marked 'private'.
Neither May Ashby's solicitor nor the coroner believed that it disclosed 'enough
to bring in a verdict of suicide'.[3] An open verdict on his death was recorded by
the coroner. Ashby was 56.

Had he simply opened the carriage door, mistaking it for the toilet, as some
have suggested, or on this spring morning did Ashby commit suicide?[4] He had
plenty enough motive to end his life.

Academics can rarely be brought back to life by biographers. By nature
they are cerebral creatures whose habitat is the library, whose adventures are few,
and whose manner is generally unremarkable. Ashby is no exception, and yet his

life was not without incident, not least because he energetically filled all his waking hours. Like Arthur Evans or Leonard Woolley, he belonged to the transition between Victorian antiquarianism and twentieth-century scientific archaeology, well aware that his research touched critically upon a great chapter in world history.

Death flushed out the real Ashby. No longer was he the gruff, awkward scholar, but someone who had enriched many friendships: 'inglesi di nascita e di nazionalità, ma romano per lunga residenza e per sentimento di amore alla nostra città ed ai ricordi della sua passata grandezza'.[5] As we shall see, friendship was fundamental to his academic success.

How are we to picture him? He was of medium height with a lean but sturdy physique. A sketch of him drawn by Miss E. Money when he was 21, in 1895, reveals fine, boyish, features that suggest the vulnerability of an only child. Later he photographed well (Fig. 1). His eyes trapped the camera in the manner of a matinée actor.[6] Indeed, there is a touch of vanity about him, almost as though he was looking into a mirror rather than at a camera with a painfully slow shutter speed. He had bright, penetrating eyes and, after the turn of the century, a well-trimmed beard. The beard, like his hair, was flaming red in early years, but it began to turn grey in his late 30s. In his 40s the beard lent him a certain gravitas, worthy of a Victorian antiquarian or poet. The beard, it seems, was a response to the executive challenges of the British School, grown around 1904–6, perhaps to conceal his own misgivings.

He took trouble over his appearance. Most photographs show him in his walking gear — an idiosyncratic fashion that others recalled long after his death (see below) (Fig. 2). But pictured in family groups, he seemed particularly fond of a stunted tie, Norfolk suits and shoes. On Malta, digging in the sun, he wore a white topi and sunglasses. The photographs convey an unstuffy man, with a sharp understanding of his context and an appreciation that it was better to smile genially upon life. Numerous memoirs breathe life into the mute pictures.

First, here is a formal view from a letter, published in *The Times* of 26 May 1931, from Dr Gilbert Bagnani and Professor Giuseppe Lugli, in response to the obituary already published, giving an 'Italian' tribute:

> To us he was far more a fellow Roman than the Director of a foreign school. He was respected for his unrivalled knowledge of the past history of our city; he was loved for his understanding of our modern life. He continued and enriched, by ties extending all over our country, that century-old tradition in collaborative study between English and Roman antiquaries, being in this the successor and heir of Nibby and Gell, De Rossi and Stevenson. Further, his extraordinary tact, appreciated but little by the outside world, allowed him to take an ever helpful part in scientific controversies, and yet to remain on affectionate terms with all the parties concerned. His courtesy and generosity in offering to every

Fɪɢ. 1. Thomas Ashby (1874–1931).
(British School at Rome Archive 143)

serious student his extremely valuable library, his extensive and
varied knowledge, and his rich personal experience found few
parallels in his profession; while the scrupulous integrity of his
relations with his colleagues made his home the natural centre of
discussion and exchange of ideas. His readiness to help was only·
equalled by his willingness to acknowledge the work of others.
These were some of the virtues which made Ashby a great
ambassador of British scholarship. There can be few Italian
archaeologists, young or old, who have not appealed to Ashby and
been amply rewarded. As master, colleague, and friend, *quel caro
Ashby* will be no less mourned in Italy than in his native land.

FIG. 2. Thomas Ashby in walking gear.
(British School at Rome Archive Neg. No. LVI,27)

Thomas Ashby was never an exile from his native land in the sense that Norman Douglas or D.H. Lawrence, for example, both of whom lived in Italy, were.[7] Italy was Ashby's home; but he was as comfortable with the English as he was with Italians.

In a less formal manner, the same impression of Ashby survives in other memoirs and in his photographic albums. His friend from Oxford days, R.R. Campbell, with whom he holidayed at St Margaret's Bay every year before the First World War, provided one of Ashby's obituarists with this reminiscence:[8]

> We had an open-deck sailing boat, called Bob-Tit after our joint names, in which we had many adventures, for Titus was reckless and absolutely without fear. In the summer of 1907 we were capsized near the Goodwins and, after about an hour in the water,

were picked up by some Deal boatmen, who behaved rather scandalously. They threw away all our tackle which we had laboriously collected ... and insisted on towing us to Deal Pier, in order that they might receive the plaudits of the crowd. Then for the first time I saw Titus really angry. He stood up, his beard dripping with brine, and in plain blunt language told them that unless they landed us at once they would not get a penny more than they were legally entitled to. He had always heard good things said of the Deal boatmen, but this conduct had changed his mind. The boatmen were thoroughly cowed, and landed us at once.

G.H. Hallam, the son-in-law of Ashby's earliest archaeological mentor, F.A. Searle (the owner of the Roman and later monastic site of Sant'Antonio, Tivoli), recalled him as always the same: 'the most honest, faithful and unselfish of friends, as pathetically tender-hearted as he was outspoken and blunt in manner'.[9]

From his last days comes E.M. Winslow's vivid recollection published 25 years after Ashby's death:[10]

Returning to Rome in March–April 1931 ... I set about with more serious intent to explore the aqueducts. But I needed a guide. Upon enquiry at our pensione in Rome ... I was told by a Polish lady archaeologist that she knew of only one person in the great city who knew anything about the aqueducts, and that he was an Englishman, name of Ashby ... Still innocent, still expecting to find a footloose Englishman who amused himself showing people the aqueducts, I drove to the address on Via Vincenzo Bellini. It was a sizeable house in a new development near the Borghese Gardens, and not at all the sort of place I had expected to find. And to add to my confusion, now turned to embarrassment, I was met at the door by a bearded gentleman who looked like Andrew Carnegie, but proclaimed his identity by saying, 'I'm Ashby, come in; come back to my study'. Even before we reached the study I was sputtering that there must be some mistake here, as I had expected to find a guide; but before I could even pronounce the *ide* my host exclaimed that 'They're no good. You're lucky to get hold of me; I'm the world's leading authority on these things'. Maps were on the wall, books were all about, and on the desk was a manuscript at least a foot thick. 'This', said Ashby, 'is the result of twenty-five years' work; it's my book on the aqueducts'.

By this time I had confessed, or apologized, that I was not an archaeologist but an economist. And of course Dr. Thomas Ashby, former Director of the British School in Rome, long ago an authority on the topography of the Roman *campagna,* and now the world's greatest authority on the aqueducts, kindly wanted to know how I happened to be interested in 'these old things'. Back in the States, I told him, I had been giving a university course in Public Utilities ... I related that a few years before I had heard a very fine lecture, with lantern slides, on the aqueducts. At this

disclosure, Ashby really sat up and took notice. 'Who was the
lecturer?' That I could not remember, nor even what the lecturer
looked like, for, after all, the lecture was given mostly in the dark.
'Where did you hear the lecture?' Ashby pursued. 'At the
University of Iowa', I replied, at which Ashby faintly shouted,
'I'm the fellow'.

On 7 April Winslow picked Ashby up; Winslow brought biscuits, Ashby a
flask of tea. It was a typical Ashby expedition, one that evidently lingered forever
with the American, as such simple walking expeditions conquered the
imagination of many other companions. Six weeks later Winslow read of his
death. 'Ashby had seemed to me more like Methuselah, mainly on account of his
beard. He was short and stocky, gruff and abrupt in manner, but most friendly
behind this facade.'

A.H. Smith, a founder member of the British School at Rome, chairman of
its Faculty of Archaeology, History and Letters, and, for a while, Director of the
School (1928–30), recounted that Ashby had 'a distinct gift for humorous
narration (emphasized at appropriate points by a slight drawl) … In his speech
and thought there was a straightforward simplicity and directness which found
expression in a curiously individual manner'.[11] John Ward-Perkins, Director of
the School between 1945 and 1974, evidently heard rather more vivid accounts of
Ashby's style: a 'flow of impeccably idiomatic Italian spoken in an accent which
to his dying day remained obstinately British', not, in fact, so different from
Ward-Perkins's own style![12] Bernard Ashmole, Ashby's successor as Director,
recalled that 'it was amusing to hear him instructing — or rebuking — a servant
in splendid classical cadences; and his Italian colleagues laughed in a kindly way
at what they called his 'lingua Asbeiana''.[13] R.T. Warner was more colourful
still:[14]

> … he was in his heart a Peter Pan who had never quite outgrown
> his boyhood. Hence his curt jaunty boyish way of expressing
> himself. He was fond of responding to remarks with an abrupt
> adverb — 'Decidedly!', 'Obviously!' [or perhaps more often
> 'Absolutely!'], or with some familiar Greek or Latin exclamation …
>
> His somewhat shaggy form of conversation sometimes led
> people who did not know him well to think him rather brusque and
> rough, but it was really only a mannerism natural to one who had
> no use for verbiage or ceremony. As a matter of fact he was of a
> very sympathetic disposition, and genuinely concerned himself
> about anything which he considered a hardship or an injustice.

Giuseppe Lugli, one of Italy's leading archaeologists, fifteen years after
Ashby's death, published a lyrical memoir of his former mentor.[15] He begins
and ends his account of walking with Ashby in the Sabina in 1927 (when Ashby
was in his 50s and Lugli was a young man) as follows:

Knowledgeable, like no-one else, of the countryside and of monuments, tireless walker, simpaticissimo companion, without pretensions and always happy wherever we stopped to eat and sleep, without envy and jealousy, but generous with information and tuition towards all those seeking help from him.

The memory of Thomas Ashby lives on with all who knew him: classically English, with a well-cut beard, always distinct and correct. When he went in the country he dressed in a grey outfit with wool socks and mountain boots, a wool sweater even in summer, a hat and neck scarf. He carried his camera, and a string bag in which he kept his map, food for the day, his binoculars, a tape-measure, another sweater, a small flask of whisky — that normally he did not drink, though I did — a candle, an electric lamp, and other possessions. Summer and winter he also carried a green umbrella of the type used by peasants, fastened to his shoulder-belt with string, and often sun-glasses: he seemed like the brigand Gasperone. In this get-up he arrived one September Sunday at Castel Gandolfo, on the village feast-day, when the villagers were dressed up in their best finery. Imagine the criticism; I had to explain that beneath this bandit's attire was concealed a great archaeologist of world fame …

You died too soon, dear friend, and such a tragic death: your goodness and your learning merited a longer life and a more mythical end!

Other 'snapshots' are less flattering. Gertrude Bell, the intrepid Middle Eastern archaeologist, on a visit to Rome recalls Ashby trailing behind the formidable Mrs Eugénie Strong, his Assistant Director, as her *cicerone* (guide).[16] The implication was that Eugénie Strong — the well-connected great lady with a salon of international repute — called the tune, and Ashby merely danced as required. Ralegh Radford, a student in medieval studies in 1922, remembered Eugénie Strong as the great figure in the School, while Ashby was aloof and formal. Radford recollected that Ashby was self-centred, though helpful in office hours, and that he affected to despise medieval matters. Bruno Bonelli, appointed by Eugénie Strong as an administrator in 1921, recognized that Ashby was a great archaeologist, but felt that he was a little distant in the School. Ashby spoke rarely with the School's staff. The young German scholar Richard Krautheimer encountered them in about 1928; his impression was similar to Radford's. This led Peter Wiseman to conclude that 'Ashby was a great scholar, but he was never meant to be the warden of a student residence'.[17] The letters of the young painter Winifred Knights, a scholar at the School, shed a different light on Ashby and his relationship with students:[18]

13 November 1920
... the archeologists [sic] get my goat they are all so darned
superior, & clever they always talk shop and never never play
unless it is college songs on the piano. They are not alive, they are
walking with their heads turned the wrong way ...

Friday 4 February 1921 xiv
Miss Gill & Gill went to a dance last night but I cried off because I
felt tired ... But no rest for me for Dr. Ashby came in after dinner
& insisted on being taught to dance & the task fell to me. He is one
of those people who have no idea of dancing & never will have,
but he was so keen & I really think he made great improvement
dancing during the evening but I am feeling stiff this morning in
consequence. I only pray he doesnt [sic] ask me for too many
dances this afternoon.

Fig. 3. Otto Voelkers, Ashby and Esther Van Deman flying over Rome. *(American Academy
in Rome Photographic Archive Neg. No. 28566) (Reproduced courtesy of the American
Academy in Rome)*

    No image captures the real Ashby better than a posthumous caricature by
Otto Voelkers, dated 1932, which depicts the redoubtable Esther Van Deman, the
American classical archaeologist, and a grey-bearded Ashby together on a book,
as if it were a magic carpet floating over the aqueducts snaking their way into
Rome (Fig. 3); Ashby points downwards, Van Deman makes notes.[19] This

FIG. 4. Huts constructed of wood and straw at Terracina, 18 March 1902 (detail).
(British School at Rome Archive Neg. No. IV,17)

celestial cartoon, though an image of Ashby's final years, belongs in spirit to the carefree days before the First World War, when the British and American Archaeological Society made its excursions across the Roman Campagna, and before Fascism cast its shadow over Italy.

Like many academics, Ashby was not a worldly man. As we shall see (Chapter Two), he was an only child of a Quaker family, a product of Winchester and Oxford, and in some senses a perpetual student. His photographic albums betray a wistful, if restrained, Victorian regard for women. Evidently attractive women were drawn to him. Nevertheless, until he married in 1921, he was strongly attached to his parents, and indeed after his father's death in 1906 he lived with his mother in a hotel in Rome until the British School at Rome in the Valle Giulia was built in 1916.[20] His life revolved around people, places and the past. Into these he poured his extraordinary energy.

His photographic albums chart his journeys, criss-crossing Europe from an early age. Casually-taken shots of mountains, archaeological sites and street scenes are intermittently interrupted by carefully posed portraits of his family or friends (Figs 4 and 5). Overall there is a sense of urgency in his travelling. Before 1918, he never spent the summer in Rome. Eugénie Strong attributed his summer travels to his dislike of the heat: 'Dr. Ashby … hates the heat of Rome in summer', she told Evelyn Shaw in a letter of 5 August 1916. The reality was a restlessness revealed in any of the reports for the British School at Rome during his directorship. Seldom was the School to witness such purpose. The report for the session 1909–10 (he had been Director for three years by this time) provides a typical illustration:[21]

FIG. 5. The gothic arch of the Palazzo Venditti, Terracina, with market stalls below, 1903.
(British School at Rome Archive Neg. No. VI,79)

The Director ... returned to Rome on Oct. 1st. and remained
there until April 17th. In addition to the general management of the
School and the direction of the Students, his time was mainly
occupied with the preparation for the press of Section II of his work
on the Classical Topography of the Via Latina, with the editing of
Volume V of the *Papers* of the School, and with the investigation of
the provenances of the objects described in the Capitoline
Catalogue. He also wrote a short article (not yet printed) as a
supplement to the text of Volume II of the *Papers*.

Besides visits to the portion of the Campagna and the Alban
Hills traversed by the Via Latina, he made a short excursion at
Christmas to Orbetello and Western Etruria, and at Easter (with
Mr. O.L. Richmond) he explored the coast of Latium between
Laurentum and Antium. On leaving Rome in April he at first
accompanied Mr. George Macauley Trevelyan in a cycling tour
through Calabria to Reggio. Though not many remains of antiquity
were observed except at Locri — that no traces of the ancient Via
Popillia appeared to exist was especially disappointing — an
extremely interesting survey of the natural characteristics and
scenery of the lower part of the Italian peninsula was gained. He
thence proceeded to Crete, visiting Knossos, Phaestos, Gournia,
Psyra, Mochlos, etc. and devoting some attention to the remains of
the Roman period. Thence he went to Malta by way of Tripoli, and
returned to England in July, spending some time in the libraries of
Windsor Castle and Eton College and in further work at Caerwent.

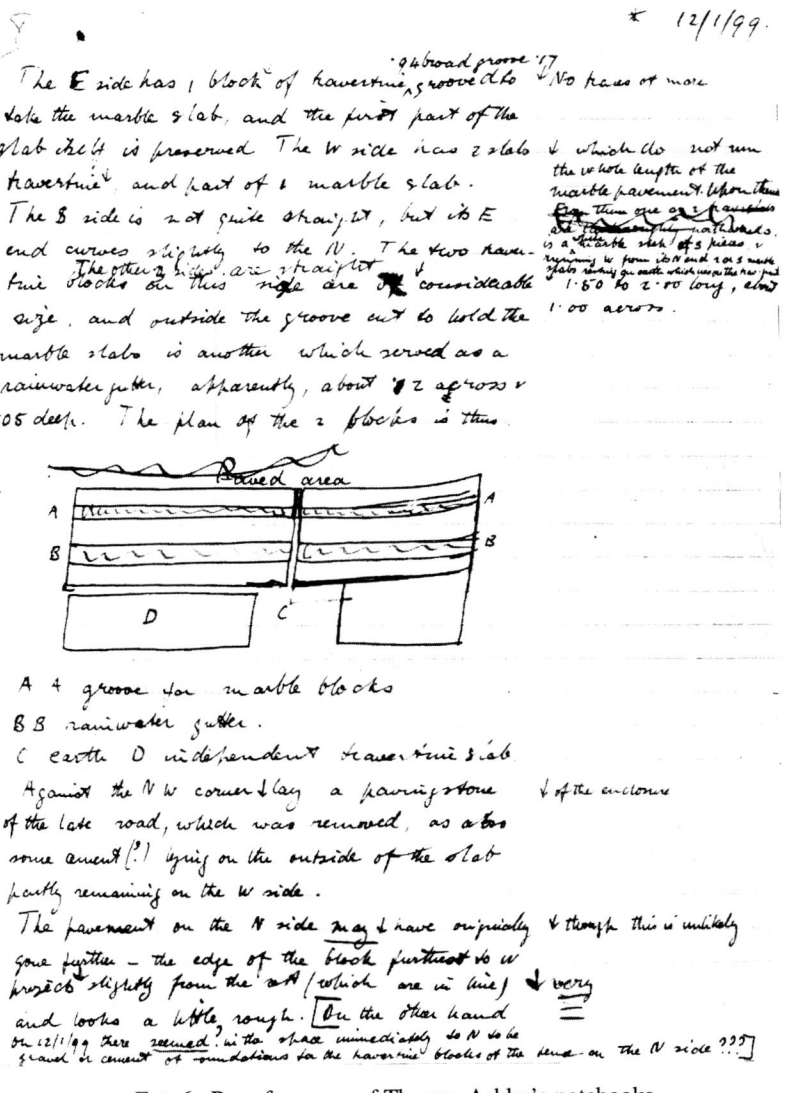

FIG. 6. Page from one of Thomas Ashby's notebooks.
(British School at Rome Archive)

All the time Ashby was writing. He was a compulsive sender of postcards. Frequently he scribbled over the picture. Always, though, his monogram occupied a neat, carefully studied, corner, as if it were a brick-stamp. His notebooks betray the same hyperactive life. His jottings were always untidy. Invariably they were ticked off later, when the information has been incorporated into an essay. Backs of envelopes, old fliers for lectures, old manuscripts — everything was plundered for scribbling. Paper was never wasted. His excavation and field notebooks reveal the same tendency:[22] a thought recorded, a sketch to illustrate the observation — everything hurriedly scribbled down (Fig. 6). His preparation of a manuscript for a typist was idiosyncratic. He usually wrote on the left-hand side of the page only, leaving the right-hand half free for additions and notes.[23] The notes are added, as he chanced upon them, in different inks. His copies of his publications possess the same annotations. Down the margins, in his eager and flowing script, are his additions. Barely a page of his copies of the *Papers* containing his articles on the Roman Campagna are free of these remarks.[24] The breadth of his interests was extraordinary. Volume six of the *Papers*, edited by Ashby, contained a 126-page collaborative report on the excavations of megalithic buildings in Malta and Gozo, his 25-page addendum to his earlier book-length study of the Renaissance artist Andreas Coner (see Chapter Two), and a twenty-page biography of the eighteenth-century collector, Thomas Jenkins. That year (1913) he had a short article on two Roman bridges in *The Builder*, an article on the Alban Hills in *The Quarterly Review*, a note on Italian excavations in *The Year's Work in Classical Studies*, a two-page introduction to M.H.U. Hogarth's book *The Fountains of Rome*, and a report on the Roman remains of Velletri in the *American Journal of Archaeology*. It was an average output.

THE WALKER

In *Who's Who* Ashby recorded that walking was his principal pastime (Fig. 7). His photographic albums record his frequent expeditions into the countryside around Rome. At that time, the city was still largely contained by the third-century Aurelian Walls. Around it, up until the First World War, lay open country that reached to the Tolfan Hills north of Rome, to Tivoli on the east side, to the Alban Hills on the south, and to the sea at Ostia, on the west. Shepherds commonly brought their flocks down to the city in winter, and it was not unusual to see sheep being driven through the streets. Rome was adjusting to its restored role as capital city. Initially, Ashby's walking expeditions were commonly in the company of members of the British and American Archaeological Society, but after the First World War he tended to be accompanied by scholars from the British School, as well as by old friends. Companionship on his walks was important, as he indicated so evocatively in his dedication of his edition of the *Mappa della Campagna Romana del 1547 di Eufrosine della Volpaia* (1915): 'I should like to dedicate this volume to all those friends who, on hot and chilly days, in good and bad weather, were pleasing and welcome company on my various excursions in this most beautiful region, a worthy crown for the Eternal City'.

He wrote little about this pleasure, but it is appropriate to gauge some of his feelings from an essay by George Trevelyan (a walking companion), entitled 'Walking':[25]

FIG. 7. Thomas Ashby with a group of friends on a walking and climbing trip in
the Alps in 1894. *(British School at Rome Archive Neg. No. TA 303)*

Central Italy is a paradise for the walker ... It is a land of hills and
mountains, unenclosed, open in all directions to the wanderer at
will, unlike some British mountain game-preserves ... The
peasants are kind and generous to the wayfarer ... The pleasure of
losing your way on those hills leads to a push over broken ground
to a glimmer of light that proves to come from some lonely
farmstead, with the family gathered round the burning brands, in
honest, cheerful poverty. They will, without bargain or demur,
gladly show you the way across the brushwood moor, till the lights
of Gubbio are seen beckoning down in the valley below.

For Trevelyan the essence of walking was not the physical exertion but the
solitude and silence which went with it. Walking was the means by which a man

might regain possession of his own soul, by rejoining him in sacred union with nature. A fundamental issue, as Owen Chadwick has remarked, was that 'in three-quarters of Trevelyan's attitudes to liberty, you can feel the wind blowing among the hills'.[26] The same feelings, we may imagine, were shared by Ashby, as they were by D.H. Lawrence. 'I still cannot, cannot believe this landscape is real', Lawrence wrote. 'One must love Italy, if one has lived there. It is so non-moral. It leaves the soul so free. Over these countries, Germany and England, like the grey skies, lies the gloom of the dark moral judgement and condemnation and reservation of the people. Italy does not judge. I shall want to go back there.'[27]

In 1890, when the Ashbys moved to Italy, only 21.2% of the population lived in cities, whereas the figure for Britain was 62%.[28] Coming from Staines, just to the west of London, Italy must have seemed a rural country to the Ashbys, much as it did to Lawrence with his roots in the mining country outside Nottingham. What disturbed the likes of Lawrence and Trevelyan — and in all likelihood Ashby as well — was that by the end of the Victorian age the countryside and natural world were no longer central to British life as once they had been. Social investigations, from Booth's survey of London to C.F.C. Masterman's *The Condition of England* (1909), depicted an urban population that was impoverished and, as Lawrence noted, spiritually deprived. As Masterman put it: 'They [working men] experience no exaltation in Nature because they are cut off from the experience of Nature'.[29] In an essay entitled 'The white peril', Trevelyan condemned the iniquities of urban living — 'in its externals like one long journey on the underground' —, a world of 'ugliness, vulgarity, materialism, the insipid negation of everything that has been accounted good in the past history of man'.[30]

Ashby's love of the countryside is conveyed in his descriptions of its antiquity, as well as by his photographic record. His *The Roman Campagna in Classical Times* is suffused with 'the intense pleasure and delight that it gives to wander there'. This was a world before the 'spread of motor transit and of motor traction', traversed on foot, on horseback or sometimes by bicycle.[31] Thus Ashby's studies took him out along the spider's web of roads which, one by one, were to be the subject of his critical attention: the Via Appia (published 1916–17), the Via Collatina (1902), the Via Flaminia (1921), the Via Labicana (1902), the Via Latina (1906–7; 1907; 1910), the Via Nomentana (1906), the Via Praenestina (1902), the Via Salaria (1902; 1912), the Via Tiberina (1924), the Via Tiburtina (1906; 1922; 1923; 1924; 1927; 1928) and the Via Traiana (1916). After this he traced the lengths of Rome's eleven aqueducts.

Sir Leonard Woolley recalled such a walk with Ashby:[32]

> We followed the Roman road which for miles runs across country, paved with polygonal blocks of dark-grey tufa, now polished by the feet of centuries, shaded by great trees and dotted with wayside shrines; then over lonely pastures and uphill till in the afternoon we

reached our goal, a high-set fastness of the early Sabines. Through
the beech-woods we went on to the Fontana Fredda, where,
famished after our long day, we washed down our dry bread with
the water that spouts from three holes in the rock into a marble
basin — and so to a little village where we fain to dine, and instead
were all but arrested by a too zealous carabiniere as German spies,
and found that we had yet ten miles to tramp through the dark
before reaching Teano and our beds.

The 21 year old painter Winifred Knights, writing to her mother, records a
similar adventure with Ashby in the Alban Hills:[33]

Jan. 10th 1921
We took our lunch and started away at 8 am, caught the train to
Frascati and arrived there at 9.30 … Ashby secured permesso's
and we spent a lovely morning wandering through [the villas].
After leaving the villas we climbed up through some woods, to the
top of the hills, and camped for lunch. After lunch went still further
on into some hills which once were the crater of a high volcano and
we came to the remains of the Roman town, Tusculum. Ashby was
quite, quite happy then & took off his funny little coat and began
running down holes & Roman drains like a terrier. Towards tea
time we came down the hills and stopped at a Jesuit monastery and
found some boy priests playing foot-ball so immediately our men
began playing & Ashby joined in playing in goal … after that we
rushed back to Frascati to catch the 5 o clock train.

In her letter she added a sketch of Ashby from behind. It depicts him holding a
large umbrella; a water-bottle is slung by his left side; a string bag is held in his
left hand; and in his right-hand pocket she shows a 'gingerbread man in brown
paper' (Fig. 8). All just as Giuseppe Lugli described him (see below, pp. 83–4).

Ashby's walking expeditions, in a manner of speaking, led him to
encounter the great personalities of ancient Rome whom he had studied at
Winchester and Oxford. In one sense he was still a Grand Tourist, following in
the steps of Edward Gibbon, shaping a history for the Home Counties of
metropolitan ancient Rome. Nevertheless, like Trevelyan, he was drawn into the
moral issues confronting this archaeologist's paradise. Writing about rural
emigration, the binary opposite consequence of Garibaldi's unification, Ashby
laconically noted that 'thousands and tens of thousands of her best workers leave
Italy, and she makes but little effort to keep them, when, if she would but realize
it, she has both need of them and work to give them'.[34] After the First World
War, as the amount of emigration slowed down, the Campagna Romana was
steadily tamed, as it had been in ancient times. Ashby described this as the battle
of grain: 'The transformation has come, and continues again: the battle of grain is
being fought once more, and with ever growing success: at the same time there
diminishes and disappears the possibility of archaeological exploration of

Water Bottle

— gingerbread men.
in brown paper.

String Bag.

Ashby

FIG. 8. Winifred Knights, Sketch of Thomas Ashby on a visit to Frascati with
Scholars of the British School at Rome.

cultivated zones. It is just, and inevitable that it is this way'.[35] Reluctantly the
Victorian romantic had come to terms with the need to exploit the Campagna, as
the ancients had done. By this time, with unemployment being such a problem in
Western Europe (and effectively being unemployed himself), he appreciated the
need to manage those landscapes that had lain largely empty since he first came
to Italy.

THE PHOTOGRAPHER

Ashby was an avid photographer (Fig. 9). Almost nine thousand negatives taken
by him survive. His first photograph was of the Temple of Fortuna Virilis on
Boxing Day 1891, taken when he was seventeen.[36] He was a classic bachelor
photographer [37] — that is, someone who devoted himself to this then time-
consuming art because he had no family ties. After his marriage in 1921 he took
far fewer photographs. Who launched him on this interest remains unknown. One
possibility is that it was Miss Agnes Bulwer, an active member of the British and
American Archaeological Society of Rome, whom young Thomas probably first
met when visiting his parents in 1890.

FIG. 9. Thomas Ashby taking a photograph, with Rodolfo Lanciani, Father Peter Paul Mackey and the *custode* of the excavation looking on. *(British School at Rome Archive)*

The albums contain pictures from his last summer at Southgate House, Winchester, his travels through Switzerland to Italy, family scenes, a few snaps of his university days at Oxford, many thousands illustrating the archaeology and ethnography of Italy, as well as photographs taken on his journeys to Australia, America, Crete, Malta, Sardinia and North Africa. Most of the photographs were extensions of his notebooks — hastily framed illustrations of features that interested him. A bag or hat often remained unnoticed in the foreground, his interest being concentrated upon an archaeological feature (Fig. 10). His photographs on the whole are far inferior to the carefully angled shots taken by contemporaries like Agnes and Dora Bulwer and by Esther Van Deman.[38] Indeed, when illustrating his book on Italian festivals, published in 1929, he used many photographs taken by Dora Bulwer in preference to his own. Nevertheless, he was quite capable of imitating the portrait photographers of the age. The posed portrait dating to 1892 of E.H.G. Tatham — a young woman, perhaps a relative, who lived in Switzerland — is sensitively taken. Twenty years later he had not lost this skill: the picture annotated 'N and DW at Motya' (Sicily, May 1912) has a Pre-Raphaelite quality, the timeless reflection of the young women gracefully preserved in the limpid waters in which they were paddling (Fig. 11). Pictures of

FIG. 10. The Via Clodia at Le Crocicchie, with Ashby's camera case in the foreground. *(British School at Rome Archive Neg. No. TA 1850)*

people evidently were not treated as snaps in the manner of his archaeological work; these were portraits in which he attempted to experiment artistically.[39] This can be seen most clearly in the photographs he took on the Isonzo front during the First World War. The majority is posed pictures of his companions (see below).

Ashby used various cameras, three of which survive in the British School. He also used a small format camera which was probably with him when he died. The three extant cameras are as follows:[40]

(1) A W. Watson & Sons camera made about 1880. It is made of mahogany with a leather case lined with red velvet. It is equipped with a Thornton-Pickard

FIG. 11. N and DW at Motya (Sicily, May 1912).
(British School at Rome Archive Neg. No. XL,78)

shutter and could take photographs at a speed of up to 1/1000th of a second.

(2) A Pony Premon no. 6, made in Rochester around 1900. It is made of wood covered in black hide, complete with a leather container, and was designed to be used for studio shots. The bellows can stretch it to double its length, and there is a viewfinder with a prismatic mirror and an interchangeable lens.

(3) An A.E. Staley & Co. camera made in London between 1910 and 1920. This is of wood covered with black hide, and has a leather case. Its bellows have

compass movement, and it has a compound lens of 30 cm with a speed of between one second and one-seventy-fifth of a second. The anastigmatic Europlan lens has a length of 20.5 cm. Unlike the Pony Premon, it was used for photographs of activities as well as the countryside.

Ashby used two types of negatives: half plates and quarter plates on glass and later celluloid. The glass plates were 8.1 × 10.5 cm or 12 × 16.3 cm; the celluloid negatives were 8.5 × 11.3 cm, 9 × 14.5 cm and 11.9 × 16.2 cm.[41] One celluloid negative is remarkable for the deep cuts on its long sides. This type of film was designed for the 'Frena' camera made by R. & J. Beck in London from 1892 to 1911. The negatives were stacked on top of each other in a pack-of-cards formation with up to 40 shots being possible without changing sheets. These, with tiny bits of protective cardboard between each one, were light and unbreakable.

Ashby developed his own films, though where is not known. Once developed, Ashby wrote the same number on corresponding negatives and prints, and kept them in separate containers. In his albums he nearly always noted the place, date and subject of each photograph, though those of people tend to be indicated by their initials. His lantern-slide collection was of great significance to him, as he delivered annual illustrated lectures to the British and American Archaeological Society from the turn of the century, as well as illustrated lectures in Australia, America (as Winslow recalled, see above) and, of course, Britain.

Ashby was a practical man who mastered the techniques of photography and readily appreciated their importance for archaeology. When he read O.G.S. Crawford's account in *The Geographical Journal* of 1922 of the merits of aerial photography, he was quick to write appreciative articles in Italian that paralleled the importance of this new technique to the invention of the telescope for the development of astronomy.[42] As with his later interest in motorized vehicles, he was not intimidated by the fast-moving technological changes of his age. Yet, even by 1931, if he turned the pages of his quarter- and half-plate albums — collections made over 40 years — he cannot fail to have been affected by the great changes he had witnessed in Italy, as well as by his own restlessness. The world before 1914 possessed an unreal formality in comparison with the pictures post-dating the First World War. This pictorial diary remains Ashby's most telling testament: images of a Victorian Quaker home-life where the few posed photographs served as instruments of integrating family-life, a 'fin-de-siècle' romantic, a Grand Tourist, a scholar–scientist, as well as a companion and family man, who should have been appointed to a senior post in a British university, but instead, succumbing to his spirit and sustained by a small private income, remained in newly unified Italy.

2

Haverfield's Pupil

The enlargement of our sphere of knowledge, the introduction of more accurate habits of observation (and of more adequate processes of reproduction), and the growth of a more critical spirit are factors which, while they may lead to a temporary unsettling of what was hitherto generally accepted, must inevitably lead (and have indeed already led) to the strengthening of the basis of our knowledge, so that upon it we may build up a structure which no longer rests upon sand, but has a more sure and permanent foundation.

Thomas Ashby in the Preface to W.J. Anderson and R. Phene Spiers, *The Architecture of Ancient Rome* (London, 1927), ix

The Ashbys were Quaker brewers. Their Staines brewery had been founded in the eighteenth century. Thomas Ashby's father, born in 1851, was the fifth Thomas Ashby of Staines; in 1874 he married Rose Emma Smith and later that year they had their only child, Thomas, born on 14 October.[1] Thomas junior had a predictable education for a Victorian from an upper middle-class background. Aged seven, he was sent to Sunningdale School, a preparatory school nearby. From here, six years later, he proceeded to Winchester, where he was a Commoner in Southgate House, headed by the Rev. J.T.H. Du Boulay.[2] He progressed well at Winchester, though without outstanding distinction. While he was a pupil, the School founded its museum, which doubtless attracted his attention.[3] From this time he was known as Titus, a name given to him by his schoolfriends because he knew so much about Roman history. He evidently became a family friend of the Du Boulays, who appear in his photographic album in August 1893 (his last year) and again in the summer of 1906, after he had been elected Director of the British School at Rome. The Winchester fraternity, with its inherent ethos of never allowing a boy to be idle and its emphasis upon manliness, was imprinted upon young Ashby for life.[4]

In 1886 the Staines brewery was converted into a private company, and four years later his father (aged 40) relinquished his directorship and, for reasons of health, decided to settle in Rome. Ashby senior's decision was doubtless made because the family had been holidaying in Rome for some years. As a small boy, Thomas Ashby junior would recall, he had accompanied F.A. Searle, the owner of Sant'Antonio at Tivoli, around Roman villas.[5] When the family emigrated to Rome they were making a conscious decision to quit Britain and cement holiday friendships. They were joining the large, well-established, British community in a city that, from their years at school, had great significance to most English men and women. John Pemble has described such decision-making more baldly:[6]

> In the Victorians' quest for the oblivion of the South, for instinctual, unthinking life and the womb-like refuge of the past, it is possible to recognize the *Angst* of the post-Christian consciousness. Their desire to stop the flow of history suggests the void where there is no imperative save choice and where every choice reveals to the chooser that he is created and abandoned; free to choose because forsaken.

Late Victorian England was a harsh society for the majority; Italy, by contrast, was beginning to prosper in the heady wake of unification. Was Thomas Ashby senior taking refuge in the South? Little is known about this Quaker, except that, like his son, he was attracted to antiquity (Fig. 12).

OXFORD

In October 1893 Ashby went up to Oxford with an open classical scholarship at Christ Church. It is said that a question in the examination asked for a description of Rome; Ashby supposedly impressed his examiners. He read Moderations and Greats. His near-contemporary, Gilbert Murray, recalled his first experience of Oxford: 'I had expected so much; new lights in life, new learning, enlightenment and philosophy. I found, on the contrary, much the same influence as I had felt at school'.[7] Ashby shared rooms with R.R. Campbell; photographs of them reveal a material affluence — tennis rackets, shelves of antiquities and, of course, books. Campbell recalled that 'Titus was very popular at the House and had a wide circle of friends. He had a great sense of humour, and though occasionally ragged for his awkwardness at games took it all in the most friendly way. He was the soul of honour, and his Oxford friends appreciated to the full his sterling worth'.[8] Apart from tennis, the albums bear witness to his interest in cricket when Oxford University played the Australians in 1896.

His tutors in Greats were Francis Haverfield and John Myres for History, and J.A. Stewart and H. Blunt for Philosophy. In later years, so Campbell recalled, Ashby 'used frequently to say what a fine team they had been'.[9] The teaching of Haverfield and, to a lesser extent, Myres was to affect Ashby profoundly, mapping out his career in archaeology. Haverfield and Myres, while their formation owed much to German scholarship, were spirited pioneers of British classical scholarship.

FIG. 12. Thomas Ashby senior pointing out a layer of gravel in a section on the
ancient Via Tiburtina in the area of Rebibbia (near km 9.2000).
(British School at Rome Archive Neg. No. XI,29)

Francis John Haverfield was born in 1860; after Winchester, he went up to
New College, Oxford, in 1879, where he became a student of Henry Pelham
(1846–1907), the Camden Professor of Ancient History. After graduating he
spent nine years as sixth-form tutor at Lancing. It was at this time that he met and
studied with Theodor Mommsen: 'the greatest scholar of the European world
since the Renaissance' whose 'unequalled and amazing achievements stamp the
historical research of the nineteenth century with its peculiar feature', Haverfield
was to declare. Mommsen was in the process of creating a version of
Altertumswissenschaft encompassing all there was to know about the ancient
world — mostly from epigraphic sources — in order to reconstruct ancient
culture as a whole from the bottom up. In 1888, at Mommsen's instigation,
Haverfield became one of the editors of the *Corpus Inscriptionum Latinarum*; by
1890 his *Additamenta Quarta ad Corporis* Vol. VII was ready, and his reputation
was made. In 1892, a year before Ashby matriculated, Haverfield was elected to a
Senior Studentship at Christ Church, Oxford. 'Sharp when sharpness was
necessary, he was also tactful, discriminating, and reasonable', J.G.C. Anderson
recalled. Haverfield's singular achievement was that he was virtually creating
Romano-British archaeology — a task in which he explicitly acknowledged his
debt to Mommsen's *Roman Provinces*. His slightly podgy exterior concealed a

demonic energy. Literally dozens of articles were published by him over the
coming years, including major studies for the *Victoria History of the Counties of
England*. Each summer between 1895 and 1907 he and R.P.L. Booker excavated
on Hadrian's Wall. All this activity attracted local societies to him, while his
affinity with young scholars meant that he talent-spotted to create a small school
of active disciples. Ashby, as we shall see below, was the prototype disciple,
trained to follow and put into practice Haverfield's agenda for Roman
archaeology.[10]

In April 1898 Pelham and Haverfield visited Rome, where they were the
guests of Thomas Ashby senior. Together with Rodolfo Lanciani, the most
famous Italian archaeologist of the age, they visited the excavations in the city as
well as sites in the Roman Campagna (Fig. 13 (though of a later trip)).[11] After
the trip, Pelham spent the next two years single-mindedly founding the British
School at Rome (see Chapter Three). Haverfield, meanwhile, 'planted' Ashby
'among the amateurs' of the Caerwent Exploration Fund.[12] In 1906 Haverfield
published his celebrated essay 'The Romanization of Roman Britain' — the
cornerstone of Romano-British archaeology. The archaeology of the province,
under his tutelage, was obtaining some structure. He provided it with a history, as
well as with some understanding of its military and civilian monuments.
Accordingly, when Pelham died prematurely in 1907, Haverfield was elected to
the Camden Professorship. In many ways it was as Pelham's successor that he
became a founder member of the British School at Rome's new council in 1912.

Haverfield belonged to the first generation of professional archaeologists
concerned with developing excavation strategies and teams to implement them.
He harnessed the mighty influence of German scholarship and of 'his master',
Theodor Mommsen, to British classical studies. Not surprisingly, he was deeply
affected by the First World War and by its savage toll of young scholars. Indeed,
in 1915 it caused him to have a breakdown. Although he recovered, he was only
to live until September 1919, when he died suddenly. In all, his prodigious
bibliography of writings amounted to 450 entries. By then, Ashby's connection
with Haverfield seems to have been barely perceived by Haverfield's obituarists.
Ashby's obituarists, twelve years later, similarly made scarce mention of this
formative relationship.

Something of Haverfield's then unorthodox views survives in his Ford
lectures, published by George Macdonald as *The Roman Occupation of Britain*
(1924):[13]

> The Englishman, explorer and pioneer, individually capable and self-
> .reliant, disbelieves not only in co-operation but also in training ... The
> English archaeologist has been like the ordinary Englishman. Our
> students have had plenty of native ability and have firmly declined to
> improve it by training ... But there is a still more potent educational
> reason. Our dominant education has been classical and linguistic. Even
> history has been taught hitherto as a matter of words. There has been

FIG. 13. Thomas Ashby with friends in the Roman Campagna, taken by St Clair Baddeley, 1902: (left to right) Rodolfo Lanciani, Henry Pelham, Thomas Ashby, Thomas Ashby senior, Francis Haverfield. *(Source: Wiseman, 1990: pl. 1b)*

little care for things, and in consequence archaeology is in our Universities a somewhat novel study to-day, still regarded with a faint suspicion and occasional jealousy ... Roman Britain has been the playground of the amateur ... Roman history seems to me at the present day the most instructive of all histories ... Its republican constitution offers the one true analogy to the seeming waywardness of our own English constitution. Its imperial system, alike in its differences and similarities, lights up our own Empire, for example in India, at every turn.

Above all, he understood that history was more than a matter of words; it was to be found with the spade as well as in the topography of town and country. Haverfield provided a direction for an archaeology that was gradually emerging as an independent discipline, shedding its associations with antiquarianism, building up a network of skilled men, even if formally lacking in training, familiar with one another and establishing, for the first time, standards for the discipline.[14]

Some account, too, must be taken of Haverfield's view of scholarship at large. His personal philosophy cannot have failed to impress the young Ashby.

Writing in November 1918 to his former pupil, the prehistorian Vere Gordon Childe, Haverfield admitted:[15]

> Generally, I have a great dislike to mixing up politics and learning. At the same time, I am bound to remember that learned men do sometimes say things which upset politicians; and that, in university matters, action is occasionally taken on one ground and defended and justified on another … I fear it will remain true that unpopular views *are* unpopular, and no indignation will get round this awkward fact. I am afraid that we in Europe will have a good deal of friction over the leavings of the war … For a historian, it is a stirring time: every morning one wakes to find a monarch or monarchy gone: Europe's but a battered caravanserai.

Sir John Linton Myres (1869–1954) was another Winchester man. Only five years older than Ashby, he had arrived at New College, Oxford, in 1888. Like Haverfield and Ashby, he was greatly affected by Pelham's teachings, 'the best lectures I ever heard'.[16] But his leaning was towards Greece. He won the Craven Fellowship to study 'Oriental influences in prehistoric Greece', and journeyed in 1892 through the Cyclades, before joining Arthur Evans in Crete. It is said that he first identified the site of Knossos, but opted to excavate smaller sanctuary sites. By 1895 he was a lecturer in ancient history at Christ Church, Oxford, where in the full flush of his experiences he met Ashby. Here he lectured on prehistoric Greece and is remembered as a pioneer in using lantern-slides. In 1907 he became professor of Greek at Liverpool, but returned in 1910 to New College. In this period he developed his influential thesis on the diffusion of prehistoric Greek culture westwards.[17] It was to be an enduring model, long outlasting his lifetime. During the First World War he commanded the tug Syra in the Aegean and enjoyed a buccaneering career. Returning to Oxford, his interests became more historical. As a scholar he is recalled for three great gifts: his powerful visual memory, his gift for seeing likenesses and his capacity for hard work.[18] Ashby maintained contact with Myres throughout his life, and it is likely that his projects in Malta and Sardinia were influenced by Myres's projects, as we shall see.

Haverfield, Myres and their teacher, Henry Pelham, were to map out Ashby's career, though strangely, until 1931, they never had cause to find him an academic post in Britain — perhaps he had convinced them that his heart lay in Italy. In 1895 Ashby passed Classical Moderations with first-class honours; in 1897 he graduated with first-class honours in *Literae Humaniores*, in recognition of which Oxford University awarded him the Craven Travelling Fellowship. He made directly for Rome. There, as we shall see, he worked principally upon the Roman Campagna, the subject of his D.Litt., awarded in 1904.[19] By 1901, the year in which he became the British School at Rome's first scholar, he had been elected a Fellow of the Society of Antiquaries. This small professional step owed much to his first major undertaking — in Britain, rather than Italy —, explicitly as Haverfield's disciple.

CAERWENT

The towns of Roman Britain were discovered in the late nineteenth century as the amateur societies of England seriously explored the antiquity of their own territories. These societies were the outcome of the energetic antiquarianism of the early Victorian age. After barrow-digging, the societies turned to their classical connections. As Haverfield was to lament, the enthusiasm of these societies and their gift for raising funds for digs was no substitute for professionalism.[20] The excavation of greenfield Roman urban sites had begun at Wroxeter in 1858, and in 1869 St Albans was being explored. However, it was the work of the Silchester Excavation Fund (1890–1909) that became the model for large investigations of Britain's Roman past.[21] The fund was supported by local subscription, as well as by the Society of Antiquaries, and jointly directed by George E. Fox (1833–1908), artist–architect and student of Roman Britain, and W.H.St.J. Hope (1854–1919), a medievalist. The project drew its inspiration from the practice of Lieutenant–General Pitt Rivers, its explicit aim being 'to reveal to the world the whole life and history, as seen in its remains, of a Romano-British city'.[22] From the first, Francis Haverfield was an active member of the excavation committee. Ashby visited Silchester in 1898, photographing the excavations, possibly with some inkling of a similar project at the wholly unknown town of *Venta Silurum*, Caerwent.

Caerwent, a small village in the Welsh Marches overlooking the river Severn, was, like Silchester and Wroxeter, a greenfield site surrounded by impressive third-century walls. In the late nineteenth century little was known about its history and topography. The Caerwent Exploration Fund Committee was set up on 11 September 1899, modelled to some extent upon the Silchester Committee. The driving force behind this project was Alfred Hudd. Haverfield, we may imagine, was also involved from the beginning. The Committee elected as its President Lord Tredegar, a diffident antiquary who, as a young captain in the 17th Lancers, had participated in the charge of the Light Brigade at Balaclava. Subscriptions totalling £230 were raised, including a donation from Francis Haverfield. The young Ashby was despatched by Haverfield to direct the excavations, which he did every summer for eleven years.

Thomas Ashby and his principal collaborators, Alfred Hudd and A. Trice Martin, exposed a considerable part of *Venta Silurum*. In the first two seasons of 1899 and 1900 they excavated houses 1, 2 and 3 in the southwest corner of the city (Fig. 14). In 1901, excavating from 10 June until 22 October, they completed house 2 and excavated houses 7 and 8, as well as an area by the north gate. Over the following two seasons they completed the excavations by the north gate and located the amphitheatre. Ashby alone, who now possessed his D.Litt., wrote the

FIG. 14. Thomas Ashby (standing far right) at Caerwent *c.* 1900, with workmen.
(British School at Rome Archive Neg. No. TA 1549)

report for 1905. This concentrated upon the south gate, as well as houses XII–XV. The report for the next two seasons includes the first account of the investigations in the forum and basilica. That for the year 1908, a season which lasted from 15 June until 6 November, included accounts of the temple and of houses XVII, XVIII, XIX and XX. In the final report, published by Hudd, a footnote written by Ashby is included, indicating that the two collaborators disagreed about the stratigraphic dating of a group of burials.

George C. Boon, in his study of the Caerwent Exploration Fund Committee, recorded that 'Ashby was welcomed despite his blunt speech and respected despite his youth'.[23] A little doggerel, the work of Alfred Hudd, also a Fellow of the Society of Antiquaries, suggests that his presence was soon appreciated.[24]

Archaeologia Silurensis

There is a renowned F.S.A.
Whose value no man can gainsay,
He was one of Three Hundred
When somebody blundered
He's one in a million today.

> There is a young Fellow of Rome,
> Who, as soon as he ever gets home
> Spends his dignified leisure
> In searching for treasure
> Or writing a topical 'tome'.

However, it is not difficult to detect who was really in charge. Ashby was the pupil; Haverfield the tutor. The following letter from Haverfield to Ashby in the third season of excavations illustrates the point vividly. Ashby, it should be borne in mind, was by now a scholar at the newly-established British School at Rome.[25]

Christ Ch. Oxford 14 Sept 1902
Dear Ashby,
I fear that I cannot get to Caerwent tomorrow. I will try later. Meanwhile, if spare proofs of your plans and a spare photo of your Celtic God come to hand, I should like to see them.

As to the origin of Caerwent, your arguments are nomadic, straying from wall to mound and mound to wall too freely. Your theory I understand to be that Caerwent was a legionary place before Caerleon was occupied. The date of Caerleon's occupation is not known — Mommsen says about AD 50, others AD 70–80: it can hardly be later. Now you write that if Caerwent began life as a country town, it wd never have been banked up all round with the walls retaining the plateau. I do not see why — but I desire more to observe that the walls are late — late third or fourth century work, as far as I can judge, and in any case most unlikely to be first century work, because earthworks and not stone walls were the rule in the first century. Your mound, on the other hand, might suit your case. But that is not yet explored. As to Gloucester, I know no evidence that it was ever a legionary fortress. It was made a colonia by Nerva, and the only sign of troops quartered in it (which would be before Nerva) concerns auxiliaries — and that is not a very definite sign.

The end of the matter is this: that there is at present no sort of evidence to show that Caerwent was first of all military. Neither is there any definite evidence to show that it was not. You are working entirely with a priori considerations and that is sheer waste of time. Your business is to find some evidence or that none exists.

If two Germans turn up, by name Schuchhardt and Krüger, — both speaking English I believe — appear, be civil to them. They are to be at the Beaufort Arms, Chepstow on Thursday night. Schuchhardt is interested in pre conq. post Roman camps, esp. such as might be Saxon, Krüger in Roman things. I don't know them personally, but Schuchhardt's name is well known. I have no notion whether they will have time to get to you.
Yours ever
F. Haverfield

His master's voice is best illustrated, though, when a year later an important inscription was discovered on the green outside the churchyard, where it formed the base of a medieval cross. Haverfield, not members of the excavation team, published it. The inscription named a commandant of the Legion at Caerleon, a patron of the Silures. The text established as a fact the previous assumption that the same mode of local government obtained in Britain as in Gaul, based on a Romanized tribal assembly (*ordo*) rather than on an urban authority. Such was Haverfield's haste to publish it that he failed to decipher the weathered remains at the top in his first article in the *Athenaeum*.

The Committee prospered throughout the Edwardian age. By 1911, however, Ashby's commitments in Rome had become too considerable to allow him to continue at Caerwent. As it was, with the death in 1913 of Lord Tredegar, the Fund's great benefactor, the excavations effectively came to an end. Ashby returned for two weeks in July of that year, bringing to an end his participation in the Caerwent excavations. In 1917, starved of subscriptions by the War, the committee was disbanded.

In recent years Ashby's trenches have been exposed in major excavations by Richard Brewer of the National Museum of Wales.[26] The modern, open-area excavations show that Ashby's method was to chase walls, without due stratigraphic controls, often in an unsystematic manner. Gangs of paid workmen, with whom Ashby was on very good terms, undertook the basic work.[27] Without a doubt, Ashby served his apprenticeship as a field archaeologist at Caerwent and lent the project some distinction.

THE ROMAN CAMPAGNA AND ITS AQUEDUCTS

Ranuccio Bianchi Bandinelli described the history of Italian archaeology as 'an eighteenth-century archaeology essentially of philology, which lasted up until the First World War, an archaeology exclusively art historical in the intervening period and an archaeology essentially historical following the end of the Second World War'.[28] Trained by Haverfield, Thomas Ashby junior was the harbinger of an age yet to come. Already by 1890, when the Ashbys first arrived, Rome was being transformed as a city, creating the necessity for major archaeological research. The plan to reserve a zone to display Rome's monumental past was passed by the city's municipal council on 17 January 1887, and confirmed by act of Parliament on 14 July 1887. 'La zona monumentale' was conceived as a park in which the most famous Roman monuments, as well as associated churches, should be protected within an environment of gardens and tree-lined streets. Further excavations and restoration of the ancient buildings were regarded as secondary objectives.[29] Nevertheless, the project launched numerous excavations, culminating in 1898 with Giacomo Boni's massive clearance of the Roman Forum. It was this project that had attracted Haverfield and Pelham to

Rome that spring, and led directly to the founding of the British School at Rome (see below, pp. 46–7).

The British and American Archaeological Society had been established in 1865 by J.H. Parker, a bookseller–photographer who had settled in Rome, in an age that saw the founding of shire antiquarian societies in Britain.[30] It soon involved the likes of Joseph Severn, friend of Keats, and many of the city's expatriates. F.A. Searle, the owner of Sant'Antonio, the monastery built over a great villa at Tivoli, was a typical member. It was scarcely surprising that the Ashbys should join the society on arriving in Rome. By the 1890s the Society's membership of around 40 was dominated by Father Peter Paul Mackey OP SMT (1851–1935) and Professor Rodolfo Lanciani. Ashby senior almost certainly joined the society in the early 1890s, thanks to his friend F.A. Searle, and at an early age introduced his son to Lanciani. Foreigners were not permitted to excavate in Italy, unlike Greece, so the British and American Archaeological Society had to satisfy itself with lectures and excursions.

In *The Roman Campagna in Classical Times* Ashby acknowledged that it was 'to the latter [Lanciani] and to my father (the best of companions while he lived) I owe my first introduction to the delights of the exploration of the Campagna'.[31] The friendship with Lanciani sealed Ashby's love for Italy. If Haverfield, Myres and Pelham provided Ashby with method, Lanciani provided him with opportunity and boundless intellectual succour.

Rodolfo Lanciani was born on New Year's Day 1847, the son of an architect and engineer in the papacy described as 'ingegnere delle acque'.[32] Rodolfo himself studied engineering at the University of Rome. At the age of 25 he was commissioned by Prince Torlonia to plan the excavations at Portus, near Ostia. He was elected Secretary of the Commissione Archeologica Comunale in 1872; by this time he was engaged in excavating in Rome, Tivoli and Ostia. Amongst the many sites he worked on were the Temple of Jupiter Capitolinus and the House of the Vestal Virgins in Rome, Hadrian's Villa at Tivoli, and the theatre and baths at Ostia (Fig. 15). In 1882 he became Professor of Roman Topography in his old university, at which point he turned from excavating to writing. A flood of books and articles followed, initially mostly in English, perhaps because his wife was American. The best-known of these books include *Ancient Rome in the Light of Recent Discoveries* (1888), *Forma Urbis Romae* (1893–1901), *Ruins and Excavations of Ancient Rome* (1897) and *Wanderings in the Roman Campagna* (1909).

As a scholar, Lanciani undoubtedly was an archetypal conservative, slavish to the philological sources. His greatest strengths were his power of description and his commitment to recording the dramatic transformation of Rome in the late nineteenth century. The *Forma Urbis* remains a remarkable document and topographic masterwork — a map of ancient Rome in the fashion of a late twentieth-century planning instrument. His fieldwork, too, could be of high quality, as may be witnessed in the remarkable section of the network of

FIG. 15. Rodolfo Lanciani at Pietra Pertusa on the Via
Flaminia, 27 March 1898. *(British School at
Rome Archive Neg. No. TA 765)*

subterranean galleries north of Porta Pia.[33] He was knighted when he took
King George and Queen Mary around the Forum in 1925, four years before his
death in 1929.

'I was a disciple [of Lanciani]', Giuseppe Lugli recorded Ashby as
saying.[34] Through Lanciani's eyes Ashby encompassed the topography of
Rome and the Campagna. Nowhere is this clearer than in Ashby's last book, *The
Aqueducts of Ancient Rome* (1935). He described Lanciani's *I commentarii di
Frontino* (1880) as 'the starting-point of modern, topographical work'; his book
'claims to be a continuation'.[35] Not surprisingly, it is to Lanciani's memory
that he dedicated this tome. The long snaking aqueducts — in Strabo's opinion
Rome's most remarkable public works [36] — linked these two scholars:
Lanciani, the older, was more concerned with the metropolis, while Ashby's
heart lay in the countryside.

The Roman Campagna was still a wild tract of landscape, littered with classical ruins and eerily traversed by ancient aqueducts. Fifty years earlier, Charles Dickens recalled it thus:[37]

> The excursions in the neighbourhood of Rome are charming, and would be full of interest were it only for the changing views they afford, of the wild Campagna. But, every inch of ground, in every direction, is rich in associations, and in natural beauties ... One day, we walked out ... to Albano ... For twelve miles, we went climbing on, over an unbroken succession of mounds, and heaps, and hills, of ruin. Tombs and temples, overthrown and prostrate; small fragments of columns, friezes, pediments; great blocks of granite and marble; mouldering arches, grass-grown and decayed ... In the distance, ruined aqueducts went stalking on their giant course along the plain; and every breath of wind that swept towards us, stirred early flowers and grasses, springing up, spontaneously, on miles of ruin. The unseen larks above us, who alone disturbed the awful silence, had their nests in ruin.

Dickens's near-contemporary, Robert Macpherson, captured the same quality in his photographs of the 1850s.[38] A great civilization — as mighty as the Aztecs, Incas or Pharoahs — had left its imprint most powerfully upon the hinterland of its greatest metropolis. Few but shepherds and travellers had troubled this landscape in over a millennium. Yet the changing configurations of Rome (as Italy's new capital) now threatened the Campagna, as surely as the ancient metropolis itself was being transformed radically.[39] Ashby quoted Horace as he introduced his most celebrated book about the Roman Campagna: 'They change their skies above them, but not their hearts, that roam ... There is a great impression of vastness ... whether we look to the low hills stretching to the sea as far as the eye can reach, or to the great mountains on the other side rising far away'. Like Dickens and so many travellers, he was affected by the ruins of imperial climax 'in days far nearer to our own than we are accustomed to think':[40]

> All these memories [of antiquity] crowd in upon us, and are brought more vividly to us by the ruins that we see, picturesque in their decay, serving often as shelter to the shepherds who come from the mountains with their flocks in the winter, and whose huts and sheepskin clothes must be much the same as those of two thousand five hundred years ago.

Ashby's first published article, written soon after graduation in 1897, was presented by Lanciani to the Accademia dei Lincei in 1898. It attempted to identify the location of Lake Regillus, where the Romans defeated the Tarquins and their ally, the Prince of Tusculum. Seven alternative sites were discussed before Ashby proposed Pantano Secco, north of Frascati, as the likeliest.

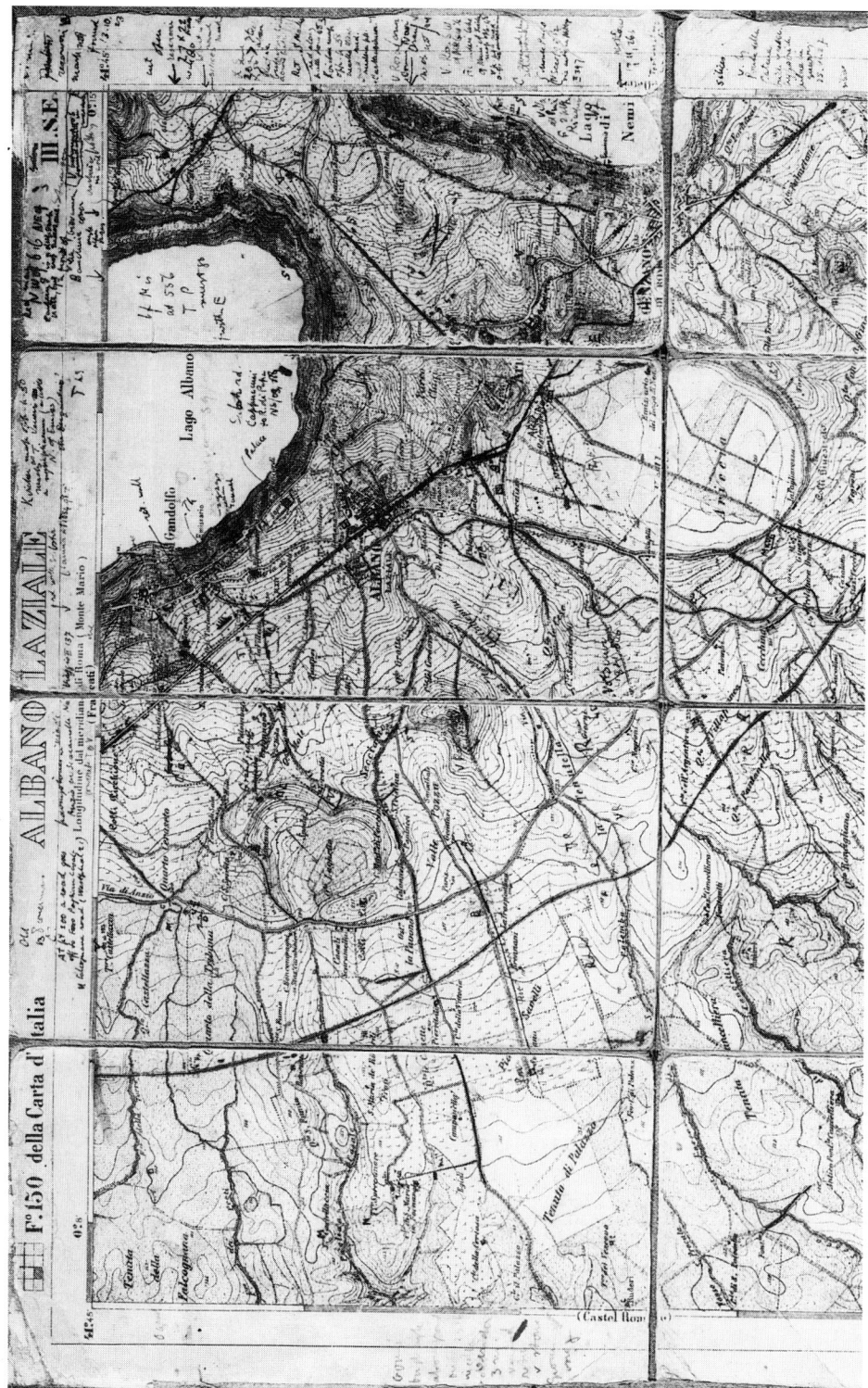

FIG. 16. Sheet 150 of the *Carta d'Italia*, Albano Laziale, annotated by Ashby (detail). *(British School at Rome Archive)*

Over the next two years, the young Craven Fellow established a working pattern that he would sustain for the next 30 years. On the one hand he focused on Rome, following the excavations (on which he wrote popular accounts) and researching the works of early modern artists, and on the other hand he looked beyond the city to the Campagna. In 1900 he published a note on four great aqueducts — his first excursion towards a book that would appear posthumously 35 years later. In 1901, in the *Journal of Philology*, he published an essay on the true site of Alba Longa. Like his work on the location of Lake Regillus, it was a sketch for his studies of the Campagna.

The first volume of the *Papers of the British School at Rome* appeared in 1902. More than half of it was devoted to Ashby's classic study 'The classical topography of the Roman Campagna — part I', which discussed the evidence from the Via Collatina, Via Praenestina and Via Labicana. Taking the roads as his means of penetrating the ancient topography of this region, Ashby systematically surveyed Rome's hinterland.[41] Illustrated with Dora Bulwer's photographs, as well as some of his own, Ashby's study followed professionally in the footsteps of his masters. The multiplicity of sources — archaeological, epigraphic and philological —, as well as drawings and travellers' descriptions, reveals the genesis of his work. Not only Haverfield and Lanciani, but also the works of earlier scholars of Rome and the Campagna, proved influential. Of these Ashby used freely Sir William Gell's *The Topography of Rome and its Vicinity* (1834) and Antonio Nibby's *Analisi della carta dei dintorni di Roma* (1837). At this time, too, Giuseppe Tomassetti was working on his history of the Campagna in the Middle Ages.

Ashby's next major report, on the Via Salaria, Via Nomentana and Via Tiburtina, appeared in volume three of *Papers of the British School at Rome*; the Via Latina was published in volume four in 1907 and volume five in 1910; and the Via Flaminia was published after the First World War, in the *Journal of Roman Studies*. He continued to publish new essays on the previously published roads, as well as on the Via Tiberina, Via Traiana and Via Appia (see above, p. 14), until he completed his book, *The Roman Campagna in Classical Times* (1927). The book, with its elegiac introduction, was the fruit of nearly 40 years' research — its few photographs are a modest sample of Ashby's huge collection. Ashby's habit of annotating everything (cf. above, pp. 11–12) is also seen on the maps he used in his researches (Fig. 16).

The sum of these works is a picture of a *suburbium* filled as early as the mid-first century BC with *ville rustiche*, small- and medium-sized farms, with way stations along the great roads. Only tombs and innumerable small lanes and paths off the highways break up the landscape. As the multistorey blocks grew alongside the monumentalization of Rome in the age of Sulla and Pompey, so the need for housing for those families which serviced the city became increasingly important. 'As Nero brought *rus in urbe* with his great palaces, so in fact if not in literary fancy there had developed an *urbs in rure* which spread away from the

ever more monumental and official centre into the *suburbanum*'.[42] Beyond the
suburbs, on the slopes of the Alban Hills or dotted around Tivoli, were the great
villas — summer residences of Rome's élite. These were places where
archaeology and history intersected — these great houses were the homes of the
Roman Republicans whose works were the stuff of Ashby's Winchester and
Oxford education.

By far the most spectacular monuments of the Campagna were the
aqueducts that had served the ancient metropolis (Fig. 17). Ashby's interest in
these began shortly before the turn of the century when, at Lanciani's suggestion,
they searched for the deposit thrown out at the *putei* of these aqueducts. He
recorded the fortunate chance that the farm road leading to the Casale della
Pallavicina cut through the channel of the Aqua Claudia. The resulting note was
published in the *Classical Review*. Several more notes were published before the
First World War, at which time he first encountered the American scholar Esther
Van Deman, who was similarly engaged in studying aqueducts.[43]

Esther Van Deman was twelve years older than Ashby. After studying at
the universities of Michigan and then Chicago, she became Associate Professor
of Latin at Mount Holyoke College. Outwardly formal, Van Deman was an
outspoken defender of women's rights, and was, like Ashby, a restless and
energetic individual. After a three-year tenure at Mount Holyoke she took up a
fellowship at the American School of Classical Studies in Rome, where she was
known as the 'tufa lady'.[44] Excited by Giacomo Boni's excavations in the
Forum, she broke with her Latin studies and focused instead upon Roman
building materials and techniques, and upon their chronology. It was an
unconventional, unfeminine, topic in a discipline dominated by men. Like Ashby,
she was a practised photographer with a strong aesthetic sensibility. Her images
of peasants in the Roman Campagna, for example, 'are documents of pride and
poverty, faces and figures depicted without idealization'.[45] When exactly
Ashby first met Van Deman is not known. They appear in a group photograph
taken at Frascati in 1903, probably on an excursion of the British and American
Archaeological Society. When she returned to Italy in 1909–10, they
corresponded with each other. By nature, as well as by interest, they had much in
common. In 1912 they both participated in the Third International Congress of
Archaeology in Rome. In the 1920s the two archaeologists spent much time
together, becoming a 'conversation piece among archaeologists in Rome', as
illustrated by Otto Voelkers's caricature of them (see above, Fig. 3).[46] The
friendship, however, was very academic. In the 1920s, having known Van Deman
for more than a decade, Ashby still addressed her in correspondence as Miss Van
Deman. Moreover, despite twenty years of formality, in a letter of 1924 Ashby
curtly reminded her, as Haverfield had done him, that 'one *must* know the dates
[of aqueducts] if one is going to draw correct inferences as to architectural
styles'. For her part, she had second thoughts about dedicating her book on
aqueducts 'To my companion and guide, Thomas Ashby' (who had died three

FIG. 17. The Anio Novus on the Via Empolitana, km 3.8000.
(British School at Rome Archive Neg. No. 2268)

years previously) and left this typed page out of the published edition.[47]

Ian Richmond, Ashby's principal pupil, recorded that Ashby was always deeply conscious of the continuity of scholarship. He believed that their work on aqueducts was a realization of the analytical approach to the history of structural practice which J.H. Parker, far in advance of his time, had sought to provide a generation before.[48] Ashby himself recalled the importance of visiting all the most important aqueduct remains in 1925, thanks to Van Deman, the Near Eastern Expedition of the University of Michigan car, and 'long days of study together in the field and at home'.[49] Ashby was never to see Van Deman's book, *The Building of the Roman Aqueducts* (1934).[50] She, however, was to see his in print, some two years before she died, in Rome, in 1937.

Aqueducts, Ashby came to appreciate, would be his life's work.[51] It bothered him, in 1925, that he had not completed his research on leaving the British School. The friendship with Van Deman clearly proved a vital stimulus to complete his project. But it was not until 1930–1 that he drafted the manuscript that was later published, thanks chiefly to the editorial intervention of Ian Richmond, while unemployed between 1932 and 1934.[52] Sixty years later, Ashby's book has stood the test of time because of the technical data assembled with his collaborators, Ingegnere Corbellini, Professor Reina and Ingegnere Ducci, as well as the architectural drawings of F.G. Newton.[53]

Part I of the book sets out the methodology of his study: the making and preservation of Roman aqueducts, the staff of the imperial water board, the life and times of Sextus and of Julius Frontinus, and, lastly, the engineering of the aqueducts. This section may best be judged as Haverfield's greatest testament, while the detailed descriptions of the actual remains of the eleven aqueducts painstakingly develop Lanciani's topographic tradition. The illustrative material is of the highest quality, with Newton's excellent elevations and maps, as well as Ashby's evocative photographs. The reviewers recognized its importance immediately. R.V.D. Magoffin, in the *Journal of Roman Studies*, concluded:[54]

> ... there have been few books of a personal research character in which errors of a factual kind are missing. This book of Thomas Ashby's, however, is one of them. Ashby was always an indefatigable researcher, irreproachable in his knowledge and use of authorities, and most tenacious of scientific truth. He is physically dead, but he will live on in his *Aqueducts of Ancient Rome*.

Ashby's topographic research in the Roman Campagna has yet to be assessed fully. The later and better-known South Etruria survey, directed by John Ward-Perkins during the 1950s and 1960s, was a forerunner of modern systematic field survey.[55] This places greatest emphasis upon plough-soil scatters of finds and debris of sites from all periods. Often it is likened to writing long-term history.[56] Ashby's research was very different. The fieldwork was carried out either side of the road system which, like a starfish, emanated from ancient Rome. Its emphasis was romantic. It was firmly concerned with a lost world of classical monumentalism, with those who had a place in history. Inscriptions, buildings and aqueducts were the principal objects of study, as well as places associated with the history of antiquity. A philological perspective of antiquity was wedded to a recognition of the need for accuracy in recording methods.[57] In this sense Ashby, like Lanciani, conformed to Bianchi Bandinelli's scheme for the history of Italian archaeology. Yet such was his rigorous practice, combined with a remarkable energy, that Ashby emulated for the Roman Campagna what Haverfield, in particular, had contributed to the *Victoria History of the Counties of England*. Under Lanciani's tutelage, however, his achievement was arguably greater than that of his Christ Church master. Ashby was the first twentieth-century archaeologist to grasp the significance of Rome's 'Home Counties' for the metropolis itself. On the one hand he held the romantic view that the Campagna was cut off from the city by the ring of massive fortifications; on the other, he was the first topographer to show, almost unwittingly, that city and countryside in this instance were continuous entities. [58]

FIG. 18. The Round Temple, with Santa Maria in Cosmedin in the background, during one of the periodic floods. *(British School at Rome Archive Neg. No. I,50 (GFN F 2032))*

ROME

Ashby fashioned his own vision of ancient Rome. As the great excavations in the city proceeded, it was difficult for him to stand apart, uninterested. Like Lanciani, his curiosity was boundless. Lanciani found an outlet for this in the pages of *The Athenaeum*, to which he sent numerous eyewitness accounts about the unearthing of ancient Rome. Ashby entered the city by other routes. He took several thousand photographs (Figs 18–20); he studied the views of Rome made by printmakers and map-makers since the late Renaissance, which stimulated his interest in the city's early modern collectors; and he himself made collections — of books, maps, postcards, prints and brick-stamps.

The reason for his interest in prints and drawings of Rome was set out in his introduction to *Forty Drawings of Roman Scenes by British Artists (1715– 1850) from Originals in the British Museum*:[59]

> All cities have been much altered in the last forty years, but none perhaps so much as Rome; up till 1870 it had changed in extent comparatively little since the days of Sixtus V, though the process of 'modernization' often went on apace — too quickly, as we now think.

FIG. 19. Finds within a Republican house near the Arch of Titus, Rome, March 1900.
(British School at Rome Archive Neg. No. TA 1223 (GFN F 1147))

> But since 1870, when it became the capital of united Italy, and quite as
> much in the last ten years as any other time, Rome has increased
> physically to an enormous degree ... and what delights the friend of
> Italian prosperity may not seem an unmixed good to the artist.

Ashby's approach to these sources owed much to his peers. Studies of plans and
views of Rome had been pioneered by Giovanni Battista De Rossi (1822–94)
from the 1870s and subsequently had been facilitated by the access granted to the
Vatican collections by Franz Ehrle, the Prefect after 1895. Ashby's first foray
into this field was inevitably launched by Lanciani. In 1895 Lanciani had
published a panoramic sketch of Rome by Anton Van Den Wyngaerde, made
between 1558 and 1561. From 1900 Ashby published the remaining three in the
set. A prodigious stream of studies ensued, notably on Carlo Labruzzi (1903), the
codex allegedly of Andreas Coner (1904; 1913), the eighteenth-century collector
Thomas Jenkins (1913), Turner — about whom he not only wrote articles but
also a book (1914; 1922; 1925) —, Piranesi (1918), Pirro Ligorio (1919), Lievin
Cruyl (1923), Stefano du Perac (1924), Canaletto and Bellotto (1925), and
Alessandro Specchi (1927). He also worked on major British collections of
drawings and prints, notably the Windsor drawings of Cassiano dal Pozzo,
drawings in the Eton collection (1914), the Holkham drawings, the Baddeley

FIG. 20. The Via Sacra in the Roman Forum, *c.* 1900. *(British School at Rome Archive Neg. No. TA 1376 (GFN F 1288))*

codex and the Chatsworth sketchbook (1916). His interest also spanned the works of British watercolourists such as Richard Colt Hoare and Richard Wilson, whose works he purchased for his own collection.[60]

These studies form as large a part of Ashby's bibliography as his work on topography and field archaeology (see Appendix). Through these collections he found a way around the impossibility of digging in Rome. Collecting became a passion in itself — commanding the archival sources at the Vatican, the British Museum, the Bodleian and Windsor Castle, and then purchasing selectively through catalogues. The Ashby collection, now in the Vatican, is one of the major compilations of views, drawings and watercolours of Rome.[61] It is an illustration of Ashby's single-minded dedication that on a modest income he was able to obtain such remarkable works. The volume of works, as A.H. Smith described to the School's Executive Committee in 1924, virtually overwhelmed the capacity of his study, and served as a remarkable reference tool for students visiting the British School.[62] The collection also reminds us of Ashby's propensity for problem-solving, exploiting these Renaissance and later art works to piece together a picture of the ancient city. Such was the ambitiousness of his many projects that many remained unfinished at his death. On and off throughout his career he worked on the Dal Pozzo–Albani drawings, acquired by Robert

Adam in 1762 for the Royal Library at Windsor, but never completed the project. Writing of his study of Andreas Coner (who now appears not to have been the author of any of the drawings in the codex named after him), Arnold Nesselrath described him as a great pioneer.[63] There can be little doubt that his prodigious energy for this research — matching the output of any major art historian — gave Ashby an extraordinary familiarity with his adopted city.

MALTA AND SARDINIA

> The wanderer in Sardinia is always getting to the back of beyond, for he must leave behind him those horrid fields of Vulcan that divide the island in two from Monti to Torralba, from Cagliari to Macomer. The magic of ugliness is there in a desolate land. But going east athwart the barrier of granite hills, he will see Sardinia's beauty where Sardinia's heart is: in Gennargentu. And if he is wise, and after dolmens or sport upon the mountains, he will always go beyond.[64]

This was precisely Ashby's sentiment. On his election as Director in 1906, Ashby attempted to enlarge the School's archaeological remit. A flier was sent out by the acting secretary seeking funds not for 'increased support of the British School at Rome', but 'towards research in the Western Mediterranean area'. The search for funds specified that Dr Duncan Mackenzie had been investigating bronze age fortified nuraghi on Sardinia, in collaboration with the Director (Thomas Ashby) and F.G. Newton, 'an architectural draughtsman and student of the School'. Meanwhile, in Malta and Gozo, 'where we are on British soil, the possibility of an excavation has the serious consideration of the Committee'.[65]

What lay behind this interest in the neolithic tombs of Malta and the prehistoric monuments of Sardinia? A critical factor may have been that it was still impossible to excavate in Italy. Malta, as the Annual Reports constantly made clear, was British territory, so it was possible to dig there. Furthermore, as one report pointed out, if the British School at Rome did not excavate there, someone else might! The someone else, in Rome's mind's eye, was probably the British School at Athens, now internationally renowned thanks to the discoveries of Arthur Evans at Knossos. We must remember also that Ashby was now Director of an expanding research institute, and with the death of its founding father, Henry Pelham, in 1907, there was a need for renewed energies. In addition, there was a conjuction of personal contacts and encounters that doubtless influenced Ashby, who tended to work collaboratively.

Dr Duncan Mackenzie had been living in Rome since 1900 and spoke excellent Italian. He was a renowned field archaeologist, being the field director of Arthur Evans's excavations at Knossos. As such he was a major figure in Mediterranean prehistory.[66] Trained at Edinburgh, Mackenzie obtained a doctorate in Vienna. His first major project, in 1896–9, was on the island of Melos where, together with David Hogarth, the legendary director of the

Ashmolean Museum, and Cecil Harcourt Smith, then Director of the British School at Athens, he undertook a survey of the island and its neolithic obsidian quarries, as well as excavating the bronze age settlement of Phylakopi.[67] No sooner had this project been completed than Mackenzie joined Arthur Evans at Knossos. Over the next thirteen years, with Mackenzie as his principal assistant, Evans unearthed the various Minoan palaces.

Mackenzie first figures in the British School at Rome's activities in the spring of 1906, when Ashby and he, so the School's Annual Report records, set off for three weeks' travelling in Sardinia.[68] It was the first of many excursions, invariably with the architect F.G. Newton. During this first visit they liaised with the Italian Government Inspector of Antiquities, F. Nissardi, and, as a result, gathered material for Mackenzie's paper on 'The dolmens, tombs of the giants, and nuraghi of Sardinia', published in volume five of *Papers of the British School at Rome*. On the 23 July 1906, back in Rome, they drew up a proposed scheme for craniological research on the island. This was presented at the York meeting of the British Association for the Advancement of Science that year, but the project as such was never published. Ashby was also to lecture on his visit at the School on March 23 1907, as well as to write a short account for *The Builder*. The promise of future work seemed attractive, hence the plea for funds for research in the western mediterranean area. Ashby returned to Sardinia for two weeks in March 1907 and sought out the British ambassador, Sir Edwin Egerton, to help Mackenzie carry out 'surface exploration' in September and October. In 1910 Mackenzie became 'Explorer' of the Palestine Exploration Fund, at which point he was based in Jerusalem and Ain Shems (and Athens when he was not doing fieldwork). The collaboration came to an end. Ashby was to return to Sardinia in April 1912, but his interests shifted to studying the island's folk festivals.[69] Strangely, Ashby and Mackenzie wrote nothing together and, moreover, the three years of excursions in Sardinia were to be eclipsed by Ashby's excavations in Malta.

Ashby, whilst at Christ Church, had followed the courses of the young John Myres and was clearly fascinated by prehistory, perhaps a further stimulus to his explorations in Sardinia and Malta. A letter from the prehistorian Dorothy Garrod in 1921 remarks that Myres was 'awfully disappointed you aren't coming home this summer, as he is dying to talk about Malta with you'.[70] In 1905–6, too, T. Eric Peet of Queen's College, Oxford, was elected to a studentship. Peet was the British School's first Scholar in prehistory; he began his research with the 'origin of the iron age civilisation of South Italy'. Ashby's interest may also have been nurtured by his largely unfulfilled study of the eighteenth-century traveller, Richard Colt Hoare, who visited the island.[71]

Yet the greatest incentive for working on Malta almost certainly was the opportunity to excavate.[72] Since 1904 the energetic Professor (later Sir) Themistocles Zammit, curator of Valleta Museum, professor at the university and a practising medical doctor, who was to become a lifelong friend of Ashby, had begun to reveal the rich promise of Maltese archaeology.[73] As Knossos was being unearthed, the temptation to explore the prehistory of this largely unknown island must have been great, for it was a critical link in the chain of diffusion, as then proposed by Myres, from prehistoric Greece to the western Mediterranean.[74]

Ashby's first visit to Malta was in 1908. He returned in May 1909 for six weeks, visiting the islands of Lampedusa and Linosa, thanks to Admiral the Hon. Sir Assheton Curzon-Howe who had him shipped there on HMS Banshee. Ashby and Peet were back again in May 1910, excavating at Hagiar-Kim and Mnaidra, and again the following spring. Then, with the great changes at the School, Ashby was not to return until May 1914, when he worked on Roman Malta. This study was to be submitted to the *Journal of Roman Studies* in May 1915, shortly before the British School was 'moved' to the Valle Giulia. Ashby made one more visit to Malta, for three weeks, in March 1921, renewing his collaboration with Zammit, when they pursued the investigations of the megalithic temple of Hal-Tarxien.

Arising from these expeditions, Ashby wrote two major studies and a number of small ones. In volume six of the *Papers* (1913), along with R.N. Bradley, T.E. Peet and N. Tagliaferro, he reported on 'various megalithic buildings' excavated in Malta and Gozo between 1908 and 1911. Along with his shorter report on the 1921 excavations at the temple of Hal-Tarxien, this was Ashby's main venture in prehistoric archaeology.[75] It has proved to be a significant essay, though it is evident that Ashby's Caerwent training was not always sufficiently subtle when it came to excavating fine levels in the megalithic chambers.[76] Ashby's other main essay was a long description of Roman Malta. It was pure Haverfield: 'During the Roman period, the Maltese islands, like so much of the Roman Empire, have no history ... whether they ever became thoroughly Romanised is doubtful: they are still, perhaps, one of the most unchanged races in Europe'.[77]

* * *

Ashby's eclectic interests, far more diverse than have been sketched here, all focused upon his vision of Rome, inherent in which was a fascination for Italy. His academic honours justly reveal his achievement: Fellow of the Society of Antiquaries from 1901; Correspondent of the German Archaeological Institute from 1904 (when he was Assistant Director), and *Ordinario* from 1913; *Ordinario* of the Pontificia Accademia Romana d'Archeologia from 1914; *Ordinario* of the Reale Accademia dei Lincei from 1918; Honorary Fellow of the Royal Institute of British Architects from 1922; Fellow of the Reale Società Romana di Storia Patria from 1923; Honorary Member of the Reale Accademia di San Luca from 1925; and Fellow of the British Academy from 1927.[78] Ashby's interests were little short of legendary, and inevitably shaped his relations with the British School at Rome. These relations with the School, and indeed his career, fall into two parts — before and after his war service.

3

At 'the Heart of Europe'

... it is of the greatest importance that a student should be able, by prolonged study in the atmosphere of a great art centre, to gain a thorough knowledge of the principles underlying the work of the great masters, and by that means prepare himself for original work in the domain of art he has chosen

The Commissioners for the 1851 Exhibition, 1911[1]

George Trevelyan described Rome as 'the heart of Europe, and the living chronicle of man's long march to civilization'.[2] Garibaldi created a heroic age in Italy. Its people, led by this noble man, had championed freedom against the decadent and despotic Catholic Church.[3] Until the Italian invasion of Tripoli in 1911, the Risorgimento held a fascination for northern liberals that was increased by the massive archaeological excavations that were bringing ancient Rome to light. The excavations gave new purpose to studying the ancient city, as did the opening up of the rich resources of the Vatican Library and Archives.

The earliest foreign archaeological institute to be founded in the city pre-dated the Risorgimento. The Instituto di Corrispondenza Archeologica — the German Archaeological Institute — was founded in 1829; by the end of the century it could boast one of the great archaeologists of the age as its *secondo segretario*, Christian Hülsen (1858–1935), a disciple of Theodor Mommsen and historian of the Roman Forum. The École Française was founded in 1873/1875, after the unification, for archaeologists and historians. Over the following decades the Istituto Storico Austriaco (1881), the Istituto Storico Germanico (1888) and the Istituto Ungherese (1894) came into being. The American Archaeological Institute, a forerunner of the American Academy, also was founded in 1894. Foreign academics were now outnumbering artists in the city.

On the fine art side, the Académie de France à Rome was founded for France's painters in 1666. Britain had a modest counterpart, the British Academy, founded by Sir William Hamilton when Minister at Naples. The British Academy had been supported by private donations from the likes of the Dukes of Bedford and Devonshire, as well as artists like Sir Thomas Lawrence. It was situated in a barrack-like building on the Via Margutta, the traditional headquarters of artists, frame-makers and moulders. Rome was, as John Cam Hobhouse wrote in 1859, 'one great academy of artists of the universe ... the metropolis of the painter, the sculptor, the architect'.[4] Thackeray described the artistic community as 'a broad-hatted, long-bearded, velvet-jacketed jovial colony … who [had] their own feasts, haunts and amusements'.[5] By 1912 the status of the British Academy was less certain. Edwin Lutyens, writing to his wife, believed that it had 'degenerated into some sort of elementary drawing class and some sheepish old maids who imagine they acquire Art by gazing at a nude man with pertinences improper'.[6]

The artists and scholars in Rome seem to have led separate lives, as is clear from tracing the origins of the British School of Archaeology, founded in 1901 in the Palazzo Odescalchi.

It did not go unnoticed that Britain, unlike the other great powers, lacked an archaeological institute in Rome. Writing in *The Times* in September 1878, R.C. Jebb, Professor of Greek at the University of Glasgow, lamented: 'France and Germany maintain archaeological institutes in the capitals of Greece and Italy. Why should there not be a British school of archaeology at Athens and at Rome?'.[7] Jebb pursued his theme in the *Contemporary Review*, commenting on 'the way in which English education has been accustomed to divorce the study of the ancient languages and literatures from the study of ancient life and art'. The solution was, he said, 'an English School of Archaeology at Athens and at Rome'.[8] It was a view shared widely at this time, not least by Henry Pelham and his pupil, Francis Haverfield. Training and travel went together. Contact with the most recent foreign research — especially arising from Mommsen's prodigious and far-flung influence — was becoming the prevailing theme of Oxbridge's approach to antiquity. Within six years Jebb had succeeded in part of his aim; the British School at Athens, thanks to the intervention of the Prince of Wales, Gladstone and Lord Salisbury, was founded. This had no small effect upon those more naturally concerned with Italy. Added to which, the massive excavations in Rome were becoming well-known, thanks to Rodolfo Lanciani's books and his articles in *The Athenaeum*.

In April 1898 Pelham and Haverfield journeyed to Rome to witness Boni's excavations in the Forum. In the company of St Clair Baddeley, Lanciani and the Ashbys, the two historians traversed the Roman Campagna. On the 4 April they were at Tivoli; on the 7 April, Nettuno; the following day was spent at Norba; on the 10 April they went to Monte Cavo; the 14 April was spent at Ostia; and the 15 April at Palestrina.[9] Their hosts evidently left them in no doubt as to their mission. Within the year Pelham gave notice to the Managing Committee of the British School at Athens (of which he was a member) that he aimed to bring before it 'proposals for the establishment of some simple form of organisation for the assistance of British students in Rome'.[10] Pelham was by now not only Camden Professor of Ancient History at Oxford but also President of Trinity College. He was a formidable administrator, in part because cataracts clouded his vision, making research difficult.[11] Despite his meagre research record, he had nevertheless gathered around himself a telling group of young scholars, whom he resourcefully put to use to found the School. In May 1899 a Memorandum for the School was printed. This was signed by Percy Gardner, Professor of Classical Archaeology at Oxford, W. Loring, the Honorary Secretary of the British School at Athens, the publisher George Macmillan in his capacity as Honorary Secretary to the Hellenic Society, J.S. Reid, Professor of Ancient History at Cambridge, and Pelham.[12] On 25 October the 'Provisional Committee' published its resolutions, the first of which was 'to promote the study of Roman and Graeco-Roman archaeology in all its departments, and of palaeography'; 'it shall also be ... a School of Roman and Italian Studies', and 'a centre at which information can be obtained and books consulted by British travellers in Italy ... for these purposes a Library shall be formed and maintained of archaeological and other suitable books, including maps, plans, and photographs'. Travelling students of the Royal Academy and the Royal Institute of British Architects were to be welcomed. Its trustees were those of the British School at Athens, who, according to the Memorandum, would appoint the Director on a three-yearly term. In Rome, Matilda Lucas noted the news in her diary for 21 January 1900.[13] Among those answering the appeal for support was Thomas Ashby junior.

In March 1900 Pelham announced in a circular that Mr G. McNeil Rushforth MA of Oriel College, Oxford, his former pupil, had been elected Director. £500 per year could be guaranteed as income for the School for the next three years. The search for funds became critical. By January 1901 £205 had been raised in subscriptions, including £10 from Ashby senior and £5 from his wife, while £628 had been raised as donations. Meanwhile, a circular in November 1900 called for students to apply to Pelham for admission. Two months later the School was in operation. Rushforth had found a suitable set of rooms on lease for three years, in the Palazzo Odescalchi, Piazza Santi Apostoli. The Palazzo had been built in the 1660s as the Palazzo Chigi and passed to the Odescalchi family in 1694. The plan and interior were by Carlo Maderna, the façade by Bernini. In 1885 the Palazzo had suffered a serious fire, but by 1900 it was restored. The British School paid 250 lire per month for a suite on the second floor. It was formally inaugurated by Lord Currie, the then British ambassador, on 11 April, some three years after Pelham's visit.

Almost at once Rushforth gave a lecture that, the circular announced, 'may be shortly published, and also a monograph on The Roman Roads in the Campagna, by Mr. T. Ashby, late Craven Fellow in the University of Oxford, and now a student at the School'. In March 1901 the Managing Committee determined to publish Ashby's essay along with Rushforth's study of Santa Maria Antiqua in the first volume of the School's *Papers*. The Annual Report commented that 'Mr. Ashby's paper is an excellent illustration of the work that is being done, and has yet to be done, in the Campagna Romana, — work which requires a trained eye and the most patient and constant personal examination of the ground'. By September the School's first balance sheet showed that the expenses were running at £385, of which the Director's salary of £200 made up the greatest portion (— the director of the British School at Athens was paid £500).[14] Its Managing Committee now included Francis Haverfield and Sir Rennell Rodd, a member of the British embassy at Rome; Arthur H. Smith, Keeper of Romano-British Antiquities in the British Museum, was Acting Honorary Secretary. Almost by osmosis, Pelham propelled the School onward.

Rushforth remained only until February 1903, when he retired on grounds of ill-health, prey to the ever-present threat of malaria.[15] Ashby, made Honorary Librarian four months before, was now Acting Director and 'discharged the duties of Director ... to the complete satisfaction of the Committee'.[16] Thomas Ashby senior presumably recognized the opportunity before him. He made the School a benefaction of £100 per annum, which enabled his son to be appointed Assistant Director to the new incumbent, Henry Stuart Jones (1867–1939).

Stuart Jones, a Trinity scholar and another pupil of Pelham, embarked upon a major project to catalogue the sculpture collections of the *Comune* of Rome. In October 1903 he enlisted Alan Wace (1879–1957), a British School at Athens scholar, in this project. Stuart Jones hoped to find Wace a permanent niche at the School (he was appointed Librarian in 1905–6), and urged the Managing Committee to appoint him to the Assistant Directorship when Ashby's term expired. But Stuart Jones himself had to resign on medical advice early in 1905 (so it was recorded), and the search began for a distinguished scholar to succeed him.[17]

The search for the third Director went on for some time. First the Committee approached the British Museum to see if the Honorary Secretary, Arthur Smith, might be released for two years. The Trustees of the Museum refused. Next Percy Gardner, Lincoln and Merton Professor of Classical Archaeology at Oxford, was approached; he hesitated. Eventually he declined the invitation and advanced the name of L.R. Farnell (1856–1934), Senior Tutor at Exeter College, Oxford. Pelham, however, disregarded Farnell, perhaps because his real interests lay in Greek archaeology. Then the name of Roger Fry was put forward. Fry asked to meet the Secretary of the Committee, but in the event accepted the directorship of the Metropolitan Museum of New York.[18] In April 1906 the Directorship was advertised. Ashby and Wace both applied; so did five others. Ashby was appointed for three years, on a salary of £400 per year; his chief competitor, Wace, was offered the Assistant Directorship, but turned it down. Wace's health was given as the reason for his departure from Rome; in practice he went digging in Sparta, then on a tour of the Southern Sporades.[19] Wace had a 'spare frame' but he was restlessly energetic, not unlike Ashby. Like Ashby, he was quietly spoken, sometimes blunt, but a good teller of tales. Perhaps his greatest failings in this circle dominated by Pelham were that he was a product of Cambridge and that his true research interests lay in Greece.

Thomas Ashby's appointment was welcomed by *The Times* because he had 'already made warm friends among Italian archaeologists and the directors of the foreign schools'.[20] Ashby was aged 31, with no experience of teaching or supervising students other than what he had picked up in the School. He owed his post to Pelham's patronage, supported by Haverfield, as well as to his extraordinary academic productivity. However, Ashby was not easy to work with. His first Assistant Director, A.M. Daniel, resigned — the Annual Report informed the School's Subscribers that 'though a cause of regret, [it] had been arranged from the beginning'.[21] Rather more preoccupying for the fledgling organization was the death in 1907 of Pelham, aged only 61. The incoming Chairman, J.S. Reid was soon called upon to persuade the new Assistant Director, A.H.S. Yeames, not to resign as he also encountered Ashby's allegedly blunt tone. The uneasiness caused the School to draw up new conditions of service, stating baldly that 'the decision of the Director shall prevail subject only to an appeal to the Committee'. Behind these disagreements lay Alan Wace, briefly back in Rome to complete Stuart Jones's project to catalogue the sculptures in the Capitoline Museums. (Probably intentionally, he visited Rome in August and September 1908, when Ashby was away on his excavations at Caerwent.) Following Stuart Jones's visit to Rome in the winter of 1908–9, Ashby felt anxious enough to ask the Managing Committee in February 1909 what its view was about the future of his Directorship. Nearly a decade later Ashby was to write tetchily 'I have suffered from a succession of delicate Directors and Assistant Directors at the old School'.[22]

At a specially convened meeting on 23 February, the Committee reappointed Ashby from autumn 1909, but for only two years. Its conclusions were transparent:[23]

> On the one hand they appreciated Dr. Ashby's zeal for the School and the reputation he had won as an expert in his own subject ... On the other hand in reviewing the past history of the School they felt with concern that no nucleus however small had been formed of younger archaeologists to maintain and extend its work. It was with great difficulty that anyone in a subordinate position could be induced to return to the School for a second session. The Committee could see there was something to be said on the other side, and it did not take the pique or prejudice of any individual for more than it was worth, but they felt that all along the line there was evidence of an inability to hit it off with men in a subordinate position, and this they thought a grave issue.

They intended to find a new Director in 1911. Wace was one of the names they had in mind. Strange though these comments seem, bearing in mind Ashby's collaboration with the scholars Newton and Peet in the western mediterranean project and with Hudd and Martin at Caerwent, there can be little doubt that Ashby's hyperactive travelling and researching was not serving him altogether well. Now, however, the School entered a new phase. The Committee, ready to

face up to the trial of changing the Director in 1911, appointed a new Assistant
Director, a woman.

'The Committee have been fortunate in securing the services of Mrs. S.
Arthur Strong as Assistant Director. They feel that her just fame as a writer on art
and archaeology, and her capacity for inspiring students with enthusiasm, and her
special knowledge of library administration combine to make this a peculiarly
happy appointment'.[24] Mrs S. Arthur Strong LLD had been appointed to
appease those of the Stuart Jones wing, for whom sculpture was the pre-eminent
concern in archaeology, to bring fresh substance to the School's teachings, and,
above all, to provide it with connections. Eugénie Strong was to play a major part
in Ashby's life (Fig. 21).

Eugénie Sellars was one of the first students admitted to the British School
at Athens in the 1880s. A photograph from those years shows her as a tall and
heavy-boned woman with powerful, almost masculine, features. From Athens she
went to Munich, and then, in 1892, to the German Archaeological Institute at the
Palazzo Caffarelli. She first lectured in Rome to the British and American
Archaeological Society in March 1897 and was a Subscriber to the School from
1902. Her first major book was a translation of Franz Wickhoff's essay on the
styles of Roman art. In many ways this was a preface to her own pioneering book,
Roman Sculpture from Augustus to Constantine (1907). In 1897 she married the
Hon. Sandford Arthur Strong, formerly professor of Arabic at University College,
London, and then librarian at Chatsworth as well as librarian to the House of
Lords. Strong was an energetic, gifted, man, with access to those in power. At a
dinner party in Rome in January 1900, Matilda Lucas noted Mr Strong 'and his
handsome wife who, as Miss Sellars, is well known for her lectures on Greek art;
her beauty is Greek'.[25] Arthur Strong, who had always suffered bad health,
collapsed in 1903, aged 40, and died in January 1904. One friend observed that
Eugénie's 'grief brought home to those who had known them together what that
companionship had meant'.[26] The 8th Duke of Devonshire, Spencer Compton
Cavendish, decided that there should be some continuity to Strong's work at
Chatsworth and Mrs Strong was appointed librarian. It was a powerful position,
for the 8th Duke was 'probably the only man in England both secure enough and
careless enough to forget an engagement with his sovereign'.[27] He had served
in Cabinets for nearly 30 years, and Devonshire entertainments became the
stateliest in Society. At this time, though, the Duke's political career was near its
end. More time could be spent at Chatsworth, although it was in Cannes, not
Derbyshire, that the Duke was to die in March 1908. Eugénie Strong almost at
once left her post. Her friends now funded a Fellowship for her at Girton College,
Cambridge. It was from there, being an Associate of the British School since
1906, that she wrote to its Managing Committee offering her services as Assistant
Director. Such connections, at this juncture in the School's perilous history, were
priceless. Mrs Strong was a widow of 48, fourteen years older than Ashby.

Axel Boethius, the Rector Magnificus of the University of Gothenburg,

FIG. 21. Eugénie Strong.
(British School at Rome Archive 1315)

writing in the *Svenska Dagbladet* after the news of Eugénie Strong's death in 1943, remarked:[28]

> The great English tradition in the secular Rome encountered in our generation two very important scholars, Dr. Thomas Ashby and Mrs Eugenie Strong. In contrast to Ashby, the restless unpretentious expert on the Campagna and topography of Rome, Mrs Strong stood as a brilliant personality of marked general culture, with a leading position in Roman society. While Ashby's English had an accent of its own and reflected in its quick tempo and certain Italian cadences his mobile life in Italian districts, Mrs Strong's English had preserved an unmistakable university flavour, together with a strong literary and dramatic atmosphere.

Eugénie Strong's relations with Ashby cannot be defined readily. Intellectually she was closely associated with the German school of classical archaeology. Haverfield's pupil must have been more than a little awe-struck. But she was much more besides. A large, emotional, woman, with an attentive circle of minor aristocratic friends, her circumstances were markedly different to those of the scion of a brewing family who was happiest roaming the countryside of Latium. It was a distinction that remained clear to all, until they simultaneously left the School, in 1925. Once Eugénie Strong was in post, the Committee looked afresh at the School and at the work of its young Director. In 1910 Ashby's tenure was extended until 1913; Alan Wace's future was to lie in the directorship in Athens.

The International Exhibitions held in Rome and Turin in 1911 were the ultimate expression of nineteenth-century nationalism: that in Rome was to provide new challenges and opportunities for Ashby. A pavilion was required to display Britain's artists to the continental public. A Board of Trade committee was set up, and it charged Edwin Lutyens with the design of a building. 'The condition to copy, i.e. to adapt the upper order of the west front of St Paul's', Lutyens explained to fellow architect Herbert Baker, 'was given me by the Board of Trade. They thought it all very like, but it wasn't a bit which is where the fun came in for me. The whole order had to be altered'.[29] The pavilion was erected on a bare hill, flanked on the left-hand side by those of Germany and Japan, and on the right by the Palazzo di Belle Arti (Fig. 22). Its façade was of fibrous plaster in imitation of stone. At the opening, on 11 March, the press were enthusiastic. *Il Messaggero* commented: 'The English pavilion ... claims the unqualified applause of all intelligent art lovers and gives to us Italians the best example of what an artistic exhibition might and should have been'.[30] Meanwhile, Ashby and Eugénie Strong, supported by Lanciani, mounted an exhibition at the Castel Sant'Angelo to show the influence of Rome on British artists of the past. At the Baths of Diocletian there was an exhibition on the Roman Empire — but the 'Britannia' section, according to Eugénie Strong, was a national disgrace.

The Ambassador, Sir Rennell Rodd, did not let the opportunity pass, and drew attention to Rome and the British School. He was almost certainly behind the approach made that year to the British School at Rome's Managing Committee by Lord Esher, representing the Commissioners of the 1851 Exhibition. Together with representatives of the Royal Society and the Royal Institute of British Architects, Esher advanced a bold plan to make Lutyens's exhibition pavilion into a new, enlarged, School at Rome. Through Rennell Rodd's friendship with the mayor of Rome, the anglophile Ernesto Nathan, the Ambassador was able to obtain the site of the pavilion for a permanent British centre. By 8 December Rodd had concluded the negotiations. Four days later representatives of all the parties met in London to complete arrangements for the composition of the Council, Executive Committee and Faculties of the new School. A building subcommittee set to work; Lutyens was charged with the task

FIG. 22. Postcard showing the view from the French pavilion of (from left to right) the British pavilion, the Palazzo di Belle Arti (Italy, China, Greece, Bulgaria, Holland, Denmark, Switzerland, Sweden, Norway) and the Serbian pavilion.
(British School at Rome Archive 2)

of turning the pavilion into a hostel for 25 students, with quarters for the Director, at a maxiumum cost of £15,000. His first estimates came to £40,000, without taking into consideration the heating system or lights. Lord Esher refused to sanction a public appeal for further funds — gentlemen did not do this; the project would be developed piecemeal as funds came on stream, beginning with the £15,000.

On 22 June 1912 the British School had a new charter finally establishing Britain in line with the French and American Academies — 'an institution which will place us on a level with other nations in the matter of artistic education'.[31] For the purposes of continuity, it was agreed that the tenures of Ashby and Mrs Strong should be renewed.

Building a new British School was to prove a far greater challenge than the committees in London envisaged. It was hoped that Lutyens's building might be opened by 1914. But nothing went right. Lutyens took measure of the anxiety in his letters home:[32] 'Mrs Arthur Strong is in a very querulous and yah yah mood. I think she thinks our school is going to be too big for her and she is terrified of the rough architectural students. Why she picks out the architectural ones I don't like to think'. In another letter he noted: 'Mrs Strong, who was once so keen, is now depressed and thinks the new building will be too far out of

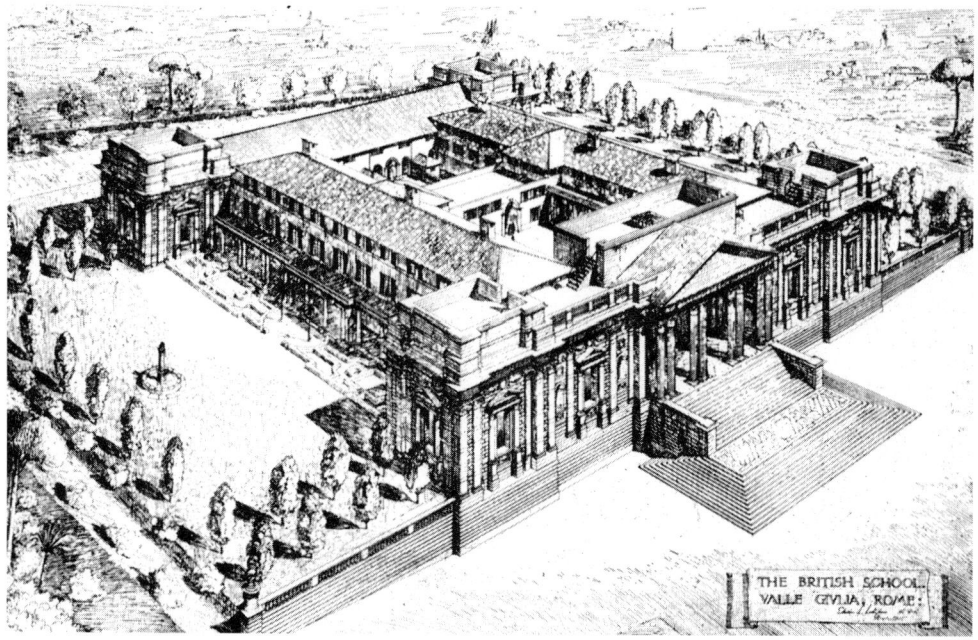

FIG. 23. Perspective of Edwin Lutyens's final scheme for the British School at Rome.
(British School at Rome Archive)

Rome — and is making things difficult. I have likened Mrs Strong to a great big
retriever and Ashby to a small wire-haired terrier that trots round after her'.[33]

Lutyens's scheme was to adapt the pavilion. The central part of the façade
was to be reconstructed and the rooms behind were to be retained and modified
for the artists' studios. Lutyens was instructed to accept the tender of £12,000 for
the work received from Colonel Humphreys (an engineer). Demolition of the
temporary façade went ahead in October 1912. As the new façade was erected,
Rennell Rodd recognized that 'unless the proposed hostel was built at the same
time as the library and lecture theatre, the work of the School would be severely
handicapped since it was "so far out of the city"'.[34] Lutyens was compelled to
revise his plans and proposed the quadrangle (Fig. 23). Not until the autumn of
1913 did work on this huge building commence. There followed two years of
acrimony. Eugénie Strong went to Canada for three months in the autumn of
1913, as the Charles Eliot Norton lecturer. Ashby likewise left the building works
behind, going in the spring of 1914 to Australia to read two papers to the meeting
of the British Association, before making a tour of cities to raise support for the
new School.

While Ashby was abroad in May 1914 Eugénie Strong wrote to Evelyn
Shaw expressing her concern about the project. Quoting a comment made to her
by 'a rich man', she asked 'How is it that all this money was spent on a façade

which you don't need when you were short of money for so important an item as the library? This question has been asked so often that I feel rather discouraged'.[35] Shaw, typically, indicated to his secretary that this section was 'private' — that is, it should not be shown to the Executive Committee. From this time onwards Mrs Strong began to solicit her friends for funding for the new School; she was the first to realize its likely problems if it lacked an endowment.

In this period, while Ashby was away, the temper of the project began to alter. One reason for this was somewhat improbable. Eugénie Strong, now aged 54, formed a powerful relationship with a young French dragoon, Christian Mallet. Christian Mallet had visited Eugénie Strong as early as October 1912. His postcard to her suggests a common interest in antiquities. His written English indicates an English education. By 1914, during Ashby's absence, their relationship had blossomed. In an unworldly 'envoi' of 27 February 1915, Eugénie Strong recounted how 'I always like to remember how we smuggled you, a French subject, into our British School in the guise of honorary assistant secretary'. The Palazzo Odescalchi staff must have been amazed. She continued, 'from the first I preferred to call you my adopted son, as by a premonition that we should be united always in a common love of Rome, and this confidence of mine was never betrayed, for Rome in her every aspect found you responsive'. She then described their travels together:

> Do you remember that Easter Eve on the Via Appia when a great red moon lay in a hollow of the Alban hills? ... Do you ever think of the little flat on the Monte Tarpeo, and of the view, perhaps the noblest in the world, which would at times be lifted by music beyond the conditions of time and space? ... Little did either of us guess that when I revised the lectures [*Apotheosis and the After-life*] for publication it would be during weeks of alternating hopes and fears, relieved by trust in the alliance of your country and of mine in the cause of liberty, lit up by the brave confidence of your letters which confirmed what we already knew in our hearts of the valour of yourself and your Dragoons. On that fateful night of July 31st you had ridden out of Reims with France's vanguard a simple Cavalier; since then you have twice won promotion. It is with affectionate pride, therefore, that I inscribe beneath your name the grade you have won by an act of great bravery on the battlefield. Once again have you proved yourself worthy to serve in one of the proudest regiments of France.

A postcard from Rouen sent by Mallet to Mrs Strong, possibly in the summer of 1915, began 'Dearest — all heart-greetings'. In common with most of Europe, Mrs Strong was emotionally propelled into the savage war that engulfed the continent.[36]

By the middle of 1915 the building works were far behind. As most of the materials were brought out from Britain, delays were inevitable. Indeed one consignment of cast-iron pipes never arrived, being lost when the SS Bittern was torpedoed. Rennell Rodd lost his temper with the project, threatening to resign from the Council if the building was not finished by 30 July. Lutyens, stung into action, came to see for himself. Lord Esher's local architect was at odds with the builder; the builder was at odds with the contractors; Ashby and Strong, meanwhile, were bombarding Evelyn Shaw, the new Secretary to the British School in London, with anxious accounts.[37] Ashby accompanied Lutyens to all his meetings; Lutyens felt he was being chaperoned unnecessarily; Ashby complained that he knew the people concerned and it was through his connection that Lutyens was able to get so much achieved. Meanwhile Lutyens noted: 'I saw Mrs Strong who was v. meek and mild ... I suppose the reaction to a storm!!'.[38]

On 26 June 1915 Ashby felt compelled to tell Evelyn Shaw roundly: 'Once more. *Don't* give the next contract to Humphreys!'. Within weeks Ashby had joined the First British Red Cross Ambulance Unit on the Italian front. Eugénie Strong was clearly perturbed by the responsibility now upon her. On the 8 August she wrote to Shaw: 'When I left you on Thursday I felt rather depressed, but after all I am glad we had that talk, for the best way to forestall certain difficulties is to point out beforehand how they might arise'. She went on, though, in a tone which was ominous of things to come: 'I do not suppose that the advice of an Assistant Director counts for much, but ...'. Shaw received a blizzard of frenzied letters on every conceivable matter. Ashby too, far away at the Villa Trento near the front, was drawn into the details of the new School.

FIG. 24. The British School at Rome. *(British School at Rome Archive 288)*

On 30 April 1916 the building was completed (Fig. 24). Ashby came down from Udine to take charge of it. Eugénie Strong also moved in. In the end, when Humphreys submitted his bill, the new School had cost £35,500. Now came the problem of furnishing it. Eugénie Strong once more bombarded Shaw with letters, so that by December emotions were running high. 'I am conceited enough to believe that if my Director is greatly my superior in all else, I can compete with him in accounts and the running of a household. After all he has never had one, and his parents always lived in hotels which is bad training', she felt compelled to write on 13 December 1916. Throughout 1917 letters made the triangular route between London, the Italian front and the British School. Staffing details became particularly tricky. Armando, the porter, was liked by Ashby, his mother and Eugénie Strong; but Strong did not take to his wife and children. Rome itself was suffering from the effects of war. The streets were no longer cleaned; a plague of mosquitoes hit the School, as did 'deadly little insects called *serapiche*'.[39]

By 1918, though, the greatest challenges had been met and the exchange of correspondence abated. In the spring the Prince of Wales visited the School, asking Ashby (back for the royal visit) how many battles the flag had been through.[40] Ashby finally returned to the Directorship from military duties on the 2 April 1919. Then began the task of making the new School work. A new era had dawned, posing new challenges for Thomas Ashby and Eugénie Strong.

4

With the First British Red Cross Ambulance Unit

Now Ashby has a faithful friend
Who's stuck to him through life
More tactful than a daughter
More pliant than a wife —
Has only failed him several times
in days of stress or strife.

The two are quite inseparable
In fact they're almost one —
I found them one day sitting
Far away from noise of gun
And sound and turmoil of the war
Just basking in the sun.

I said to Ashby what's the cause
That you are sitting here?
He sadly stroked his beard and said
The reason is not clear —
We shall remain in this fair spot
For many weeks I fear.

I've done my very level best
Used all the arts I know,
And tested every blooming nut
And searched both high and low —
The fact remains that we are stuck
The engine will not go.

He said with intonation sad
I'm getting used to this,
For one appointment that I keep
Another ten I miss —
But sometimes when the car does go
It's really more than bliss.

> So bang the tuneful tambourine
> And strike the harpsichord,
> Lift up your youthful voices
> And all with one accord —
> In minor key a chant we'll sing
> In praise of Ashby's Ford.

14/10/17 PWH[1]

Italy entered the First World War on the side of the Allies at the end of May 1915. Relations between Rome and Vienna were coloured by Austro-Hungarian hegemony in northern Italy, where there were ethnically mixed populations in Trieste, the Trentino and the southern parts of the Tyrol. Austrian annexation of the Adriatic provinces of Bosnia and Herzegovina had been considered as offensive by Rome, and had influenced Italy in her decision to join the Allies. By the spring of 1915 it was clear that there could be no rapid victory by the Central Powers. Thus Rome cast her lot. Almost immediately she was threatened by the Austrians, who advanced through the Julian Alps north of Gorizia, turning the river Isonzo area into a bitterly disputed theatre of war.

Within two months Ashby had decided to join up. Being from a Quaker background, in some ways it was natural to look for a non-combatant's posting. Ashby explained his motives in a letter to Evelyn Shaw, the London Secretary of the British School, on the 26 June 1915: 'I have no plans for the summer [in itself a strange admission from this normally hyperactive man], and if really wanted could come to England. But I should like above all things to join for 2–3 months some British ambulances which may go to the Italian front'. Just over a year later, stung by a request from the School's Executive Committee to return to Rome, Ashby was far more explicit in two letters written on the same day, 19 August 1916. The first, for the Committee's eyes, was blunt:

> I am definitely liable for military service, as I was born on Oct 14th 1874, and was therefore under 41 on Aug 15, 1915. I am physically fit, and do not wish to take advantage of the exemption extended to residents abroad … Italians, too, it is to be remembered, must return for service from any part of the world. Red Cross service has been definitely recognized by the War Office as equivalent to military service, to which I should become liable if I left the Red Cross, and which I should undoubtedly have undertaken at least as soon as the terms of Lord Derby's Act were made public. I joined the Red X because I considered that I could be of greater service in Italy than elsewhere.

In Turin, later that day, he penned a second, covering, letter for Shaw's eyes only:

> I feel sure that Mrs. Strong is at the bottom of this; and for this reason I now tell you what I had not wished to say before that

she made it pretty clear that she regarded ambulance workers as 'shirkers', and that, if anywhere, I ought to be 'in the trenches'. I know that others hold this view, that the fighting line is the only one that matters; but Gorizia is anything but a health resort at this moment, and it is there that most of our cars are now, tho' the hospital is still further back. I have had to go up there once or twice already. Our ambulances were the first in and have carried 2500 cases in a week.

Even in anger, Ashby contained any reference to the likely cause for Eugénie Strong's behaviour — Christian Mallet, the French dragoon engaged in the fighting near Rheims, about whom Ashby must have known.

The First British Red Cross Ambulance Unit was formed by the historian George Trevelyan (Fig. 25), together with his friends Philip Baker and Geoffrey Young.[2] Baker and Young had originally served in Flanders in a Friends' ambulance unit (which had distinguished itself at Ypres), but were keen to transfer to Italy. Trevelyan was an old friend of Ashby's. He had joined the School's Managing Committee in 1910. In that same year Ashby and he had cycled from Campania to Reggio Calabria together, Ashby taking the photographs for the third volume of Trevelyan's Garibaldi trilogy.[3] Trevelyan had regarded the outbreak of war as a 'senseless issue', but was soon won round to support the principles involved.[4] As a result, unlike his brother, he did not become a conscientious objector. At first he helped the Serbian Relief Fund, then, when 'Italy's soul was won' in May 1915, he decided to volunteer for the front.[5] Because of his defective eyesight he was judged unfit for active service. The First British Red Cross Ambulance Unit was the solution. 'Everyone adored George Trevelyan [known to all as Trevy] and his chivalry and devotion went through everything — he gave a remarkable unity to our mixed company — doctors, nurses, drivers, mechanics — all were comrades', Freya Stark, a young VAD nurse, wrote in her diary.[6]

Ashby must have been put on alert by Trevelyan himself as soon as he launched the idea, because Ashby's first intimation of the idea to Evelyn Shaw was in a letter of 26 June. On 4 July General Zupelli, the Minister of War, accepted Trevelyan's offer of an ambulance unit, at which point Ashby informed the British School's Executive Committee that he was joining up. The unit itself was formed thanks to the generosity of the family and firm of Joseph Baker & Sons Ltd. Its fund-raisers were J. Allen Baker MP, Colonel Byrne (an ex-Garibaldian), Philip Baker, a Miss Popert and Cavaliere Ricci (another ex-Garibaldian). The Unit formed up in the grounds of Formosa at Cookham, the home of Sir George and Lady Young. It was a distinguished gathering. Amongst their number were the Slade artist Henry Tonks,[10] the sculptor F.W. Sargant (who by February 1916 had become commandant of the Second British Red Cross Ambulance Unit), the young classicist and later British School Scholar R.A. Fell, the art historian Roland Penrose, the architect Lionel P. Sessions and

FIG. 25. George Trevelyan (centre) at the Villa Trento.
(British School at Rome Archive Neg. No. TA LI,38)

Freya Stark. Dr Brock, physician to the Embassy at Rome, was appointed the Medical Officer in charge.

Twenty-six cars, mostly Buicks, and men left Formosa by road on 21 August 1915, camped the night near Winchester and then were shipped from Southampton to Le Havre, from where they drove to the Italian border. On the frontier, at Modane, the cars were put on a special train, which paused in Turin for a welcoming ceremony, before arriving at Udine on the last day of August 1915. In a letter to Shaw dated the 29 August from Modane, Ashby asks euphorically: 'who do you think is one of the two Italian officers attached to us? Lieut. Commendatore Nathan!'. Ernesto Nathan, the former mayor of Rome, had been responsible for ceding the land of the British pavilion in the Valle Giulia to the British School at Rome.

The Unit was based at the Villa Trento, half-way between Udine and Gorizia, close to the front (Fig. 26). Ashby described the Villa tersely to Shaw in a letter of 2 February 1916: 'We have a most wonderful view of all this part of the front, with all the snowy mountains behind and the plain in front of us'. Freya Stark has provided a more vivid description, written almost exactly two years after the Unit arrived, on 4 September 1917:[8]

> The guns this morning came through a haze of sunlight, a short sharp sound unlike last night; now (9.30 p.m.) a terrific bombardment is going on again: Trant and I went up about 8.30 to see: there was still a sullen red glow of sunset over Italy, but night already and pale stars to the east; the guns come in short bursts, like far, reluctant thunder — an angry sound. Over all the line the flashes come: ruddy and quick from the shells, and the long pale star-shells hanging like new planets for some seconds. Most come from the Hermada; a huge red flare suddenly on [Mount] Gabriele — one could almost see its shape — and from our village Dolegnano a searchlight turns slowly round and upward, inland towards us, in search of aircraft it seems; ... to the SW ... is Aquileia — the church tower just visible in the plain. Then the view is blocked by a nearer hill, Medea, which King Victor used as a kind of observatory whence to show his friends the battle. Then a dip, and on clear days we see the lagoons of Monfalcone; the Carso and its long body down there and one can follow it up, see Gradisca at its foot and Sagrado below the S. Michele; the S. Martino, the S. Michele, then a dip with the view of Hermada behind — to-day covered and wreathed with explosions; then, bending east, the Sei Busi, and long ridge of Faiti, with the Vipacco valley at its base. (N.B. The Italians never could understand why the British tommies insisted on bathing in the Vipacco, which was under fire.) The sunlight on Faiti lay just about as far as our men have reached — apparently half-way.
>
> Gorizia, left of the Vipacco, is hidden by a little hill near here, and anyhow Podgora would hide it; one sees just the tip of the latter, behind nearer hills. Then comes the Gabriele ... Behind it stretches the plateau of Ternovo to a higher massif behind; we are already on the plateau, but the S. Daniele, to the right and hard to see, is still theirs and also the Sta Caterina. Next Gabriele is the Sabotino, with green scrub apparently climbing up it; its ridge is bare and, looking like a pathway, makes the whole seem a part of the Santo ... The Santo too is bare; these three hills all have the reddish colour and one can see the seams of trenches up them. After Santo, a dip and the long back of the Vodice rises like some great animal; then Kuk; Plava is invisible behind a hill, but from the top here (behind our hospital among the vines) it comes just below the Kuk. Beyond all these hills is the higher barrier; one can only look and wonder and give praise.

Ashby's albums, as ever, served as his diary: views of the Julian Alps, Gorizia, of the Villa Trento in its serene, other-worldly context, the forward out-station at Quisca, groups of bemused nurses and ambulance drivers, Red Cross ambulances,

FIG. 26. The Villa Trento on the Isonzo front.
(British School at Rome Archive Neg. No. TA L,3)

lifeless wounded Italians, and gigantic guns. The photographs imply the seamless continuity of interest, passing from archaeology and the affairs of the British School to the many-faceted fascination of war. Ashby, to judge from his photographs, appears to have been quite at home.

The Unit's original intention was to establish a hospital of 25 beds. This soon had to be reconsidered, as the 1915 autumn offensive brought in an average of 1,000 cases a week. This was exacerbated by a cholera epidemic; a single ambulance rescued 80 cases of cholera from a building in a single night. Initially this put great stress upon the Unit's leaders, overstretching their resources, and causing the temperamental artist, Henry Tonks, to quit in disgust at their amateurism. Most disturbing of all, on 28 November, the forward medical post was hit by an enemy shell.[9]

As Trevelyan recalled, 'The Quisca and Vipulzano roads of that first winter (1915) were perhaps the worst ever regularly plied by ambulances. Deep in slippery mud, they were mountain roads with steep drops at the sides, and sharp turns … Night-driving without lights under conditions such as these was a far greater strain than the driving in Flanders mud'.[10] Yet, amongst this group there existed a great camaraderie. Geoffrey Young led a vivacious Christmas revue. Gradually in 1916 'we enjoyed inside the army an extraordinary independence'.[11] During that year the Villa Trento grew into a field hospital of 180 beds with a nursing staff under the matron, Sister Power (Fig. 27). 'The reputation of the hospital for its nursing and its home comforts grew so fast ... And in Italy behind the war zone the fame of the Villa Trento was spread far and wide by those who had been patients there.'[12]

Initially Ashby acted as translator for the Unit and taught some Italian. 'Friendly contact with the Italian soldiers of all ranks was of the very essence of our plan ... Ashby as interpreter was quite invaluable. Indeed nothing impressed our gallant allies more than the unexpected volubility, sometimes in very vernacular Italian, of the red-bearded Englishman who proved able to say so many other things besides 'All right!'.'[13] In 1916, as members of the Unit became more proficient linguists, Ashby was given charge of the Unit's stores. 'His chief satisfaction was to go the rounds of the camp hospitals and clearing stations in his ramshackle Ford car loaded up with gifts of equipment and surgical stores, which the B.R.C. [British Red Cross] distributed in great abundance'.[14]

In May 1916 there was a great Austrian offensive in the Trentino, aimed at pushing the Italians off the edge of the Carso, using poison gas, a novelty in the Italian theatre. Many casualties came in on 29–30 June:[15]

Fig. 27. Ambulance drivers, doctors and nurses at the Villa Trento, *c.* 1917.
(British School at Rome Archive TA Collection)

> June has been full of incident, both in our own circle and in the Outer
> World. No sooner did the sound of battle roll across the plains of the
> Veneto from the mountains above Vicenza than the Unit set about
> organizing an Expeditionary Force, and Dr. Ashby with Messrs. Meyer
> and Kemp set off in prompt obedience to the call of duty. The
> expedition arrived in the nick of time, the Austrian offensive has been
> checked and our men have returned to port.

On 6 August 1916 the Italians launched a new offensive on the Sabotino, Oslavia
and Podgora heights. The Unit followed, dealing with the casualties. The
offensive faltered and, from August 1916 until October 1917, the front settled
down in Gorizia. During this period, until the Russians defected from the
Alliance in the summer of 1917, the Italians had an advantage of artillery.[16]

Ashby's logbook of 1917 for car no. 95 (a Ford purchased by the British
Red Cross Society) survives in the British School at Rome's archives.[17] It
begins on the 2 April 1917 — most days he was out between Cormons and
Gradisca near the front, and only occasionally went to Udine. He visited Rome
briefly at the end of the month, returning on 6 May — 'straight out'. Most
journeys regularly ended at night in the dark. '23rd May — broke down 1 km
from Udine'; '6th June — very hot: stayed at Freifeld for tea & dinner & bridge,
& slept in garden'; '10th June — to Caporetto …'; '13th — car broke down
again'; '17th — up at 5.30 to Caporetto'. Virtually every day in the period
covered by the logbook followed this pattern.

Throughout this period Trevelyan records that 'We maintained quarters for
our ambulances in Gorizia … our main establishment was a large house on the
northern outskirts of the town (No 16 Via Ponte Isonzo) … screened from view
of the Austrians there by some fine old chestnut trees, beneath which we parked
our cars'.[18] The elegiac quality of this strange life was powerfully captured by
the young Ernest Hemingway, whose novel *A Farewell to Arms* describes his
romance with a young British VAD attached to an ambulance unit that might well
have been Ashby's.[19]

In April 1917 the great summer offensive of the Italians on the Isonzo began
with the capture of Kuk (Monte Cucco). During August 1917 a silver medal for
military valour was awarded to Geoffrey Young, whilst George A. Metcalfe and
Lionel Sessions won bronze medals. On the 20 August one of their number,
Edmund Meredith, was killed. The last week of August marked the high-water mark
of the Italian advance, when they penetrated some five miles over mountain
country. On 4 September tragedy struck: Geoffrey Young lost his leg, amputated in
the Villa Trento. Soon after, Lionel Sessions was wounded and also lost a leg.
Freya Stark recorded the following account of the 22 September:[20] 'Last night's
explosion a French munition store … went on exploding till about five o'clock this
morning. Dr. Thompson and Mr. Ashby were driving there by chance when a sentry
told them to go no further'. Ashby himself only mentioned in his logbook that he
'stayed and helped to 1 a.m. Desperate battle for San Gabriele'.

In this period Ashby's concern with British School matters diminished. Most of the correspondence focused upon incidental issues. On 7 January 1917 Evelyn Shaw wrote to him about the wages of Armando, the porter: 'You say he gets 15 lire more than he did (10 from Faculty and 5 from Mrs Strong) ... I may appear very foolish, but neither you nor Mrs Strong are the least clear on this point, so I must ask you to let me have a very simple sum for my dull comprehension'. On the 10 January Shaw's letter deals with the 'tiling of the portico'; on 18 January, writing from the Villa Trento, Ashby insisted that 'finger plates are quite necessary if the doors are not rapidly to be soiled'. In February Ashby corresponded whilst on a visit to Genoa for stores. His visit to the School in April to meet Lutyens was in vain; Lutyens failed to arrive. On 14 August Evelyn Shaw ventured a comment upon the war: 'I expect you are hard at it and like the rest of us looking forward to giving the German the knock-out blow'. On 6 October Ashby told Shaw that he was now at a new address, the Villa Zucchi, Cormons, and expected to be in Rome in November. On the 28 he was in Rome dealing with 'Red X stores'; he noted the latest news (the calamitous retreat from Caporetto). On the 8 November Shaw raised the question of chimneys. On the 22 November, from the Hotel Smith, Genoa, Ashby replied about the chimneys, and added, 'only got up from Rome on the 29th [October] by which time the retreat was largely over: of course we didn't get nearly as far as Udine. *We* had no trouble and I am glad to say all our people got there! but a lot of cars had to be abandoned, and all our Red Cross stores were lost'.

Ashby missed the retreat from Caporetto, which began on 24 October, by a matter of days. In its aftermath the Villa Trento was lost. Trevelyan described Caporetto as 'that tremendous cataclysm which almost ruined Italy and bode fair to ruin the cause of the allies'.[21] Six German divisions and a thousand guns, released by the armistice on the Russian front, were brought to the Isonzo by night marches. The Italian Third Army, with its British Units, was put to a terrible test and in three days 200,000 men and 1,800 guns were lost in a hellish rout vividly described by Hemingway.[22] Trevelyan's Ambulance Unit was assigned a new headquarters 80 miles to the south, at the Villa Trieste, near Monselice, in the neighbourhood of Arqua. But much of their equipment had been lost. The hospital section was disbanded and many nurses, Freya Stark amongst them, were sent home. In 1918 the Unit once more served on the Isonzo front as the Italians, reinforced by Lieutenant–General Lord Cavan's army, held the great Austrian offensive in June of that year, and then themselves advanced across the Piave in October, exactly a year after Caporetto. With the signing of the Armistice on 4 November, the Unit established an out-station at the Villa Trento, shortly before it was disbanded in late December 1918. During the three years and four months, Geoffrey Young concluded, 'we have carried 177,522 wounded and sick, containing the striking proportion of 40,918 stretcher cases. The cars have been driven 1,319,316 kms'.[23]

Ashby, however, parted with the Unit following Caporetto. From 16 December 1917 until the end of March 1918 he was attached to British Red Cross headquarters in Italy, based at Genoa, directly under Lord Monson, the Commissioner. He returned to Rome in April 1918, intending only to stay a fortnight, and remained until August, awaiting orders on a posting as a translator to the new British command in Italy. On 11 August, sorely tested by the heat of Rome, he was trying to leave and by 19 August he was at the Mission's headquarters. On 24 November, after the Armistice, he wrote to Shaw about housing the Ford, 'which I drove for a year at the Front', at the School. On 12 January (his mother tells Shaw) 'he has been up at the Italian front ... lecturing to the British troops and is touring around various divisions'. At this time he was attached to the Education Officer. On the 15 January he was with the 22nd Brigade (of the 7th Division), the next day the 20th Brigade, and so on. By the end of January the number of lectures, this time to the 48th Division, all in different venues, was increasing. In February the pace continued, but this time he was lecturing to the 7th Division on Modern Rome. A notice issued on 5 March listed him as 'an expert guide', lecturing on 'Ancient Rome' seven times in one week at clubs and hospitals, as well as leading a party to the excavations in the vicinity of Caesar's Camp on Friday 7 March. Finally, in mid-March, he was to be demobilized, but caught influenza on that very day and spent over two weeks in the Protestant Hospital at Genoa. He eventually returned to Rome on the 2 April, after serving for three and a half years.

In May 1920 the first issue of the *Villa Trento Circle of the British-Italian League. Unit Notes* appeared. The aim was to stay in touch, Trevelyan reminded his former colleagues. A dinner was held at the Holborn Restaurant on Friday 14 May. Ashby, though not present, was mentioned:[24] he 'again hunts the elusive sarcophagus on the plains of Rome ... Fell, possibly shortly to shoulder a large repeating spade with Dr. Ashby ... Miss Stark is growing beans with which to feed Italians, at a charming little villa at La Mortola, Ventimiglia ... F.W. Sargant ... pursues the plastic arts in London'. In the second issue, appearing in July 1921, Ashby merited a long paragraph:[25]

> [Ashby] has not been in England since last summer when he returned to his campagna. He is firm in the conviction that 'there's nothing will do instead of Italy but England — and vice versa'. Barbarossa is as active in the arts of peace as he used to be in the Villa: so the British School is full and flourishing.
>
> STOP PRESS!!! We have just received the thrilling news of his marriage to Miss May Price Williams — All his Unit friends wish him the best of luck, and hope to have the pleasure of meeting Mrs. Thomas Ashby someday.

By 1921 Ashby had been elected a Vice-President of the British-Italian League; Rennell Rodd was Chairman of the Executive Committee. The third and last issue of the *Villa Trento Circle. Unit Notes* was published following a dinner addressed by Sir Rennell Rodd. For it, Ashby noted 'We've had a busy season, and I find matrimony a pleasant state. Fell … and I had quite a good walking tour (a week or so with knapsacks) in Etruria, hunting for a Roman road which didn't seem to be there [the Via Flaminia]'. Fell himself had revisited the Villa Trento before going to study Theology at Cambridge with a view to taking Holy Orders.[26]

Trevelyan recalled that 'The end [of the war] was indeed like a day-dream. It was a 'Unit' indeed, with a soul of its own, not a mere aggregation of individuals. It left its impress on all of us'.[27] Quite how it affected Ashby cannot be told. Outwardly he was not disturbed by his experiences, in comparison, for example, to Francis Haverfield, his teacher, who was evidently traumatized by the death of Leonard Cheesman at Gallipoli, and later by the loss of Josef Déchelette, the French archaeologist.[28] Ashby certainly made many friends during his service, and he displayed his characteristic energy and commitment to his duties. But it is difficult to imagine that this thoughtful man was not affected by the experience. The Isonzo front was not the most barbarous theatre in the First World War, and Ashby himself was fortunate in his freedom of movement, unlike the young officers trapped in the trenches. Nevertheless, the savagery, all the more highlighted by the beautiful Trentino countryside, could not be disguised.

Hugh Dalton, who served on the Isonzo front, has left a vivid account of the war. Notably, the future Labour minister found the middle-class British doctors boorish and complacent: 'their conversation at meal times is about sputum, faeces, sanitation, gas gangrene and their own seniority'.[29] He also criticized the unvariable British humour. Ashby, to judge from the sources, shared such a humour, but his friends were ambulance drivers and nurses who brought a gentler edge to life at the front. For the first time Ashby's photographic albums are filled with friends rather than archaeological sites or views. His photographs create the sense of a world removed from reality. By then in his 40s, Ashby was offered the opportunity to relive the collegial atmosphere of Winchester and Oxford, but in Italy with men and women from a variety of backgrounds. Being used to poverty and a certain simplicity of life as a result of his interest in ethnography, the war perhaps did not overly affect him. What was undoubtedly novel was the constant female companionship. Numerous pretty VADs posed for him outside the Villa Trento. It is hard not to imagine that these friends compelled him to re-examine himself as, aged 45, he resumed the office of Director at the British School.

5

The Last Years: 1919–31

England is the most class-ridden country under the sun. It is a land of
snobbery and privilege, ruled largely by the old and silly. But in any
calculation about it one has got to take into account its emotional
unity, the tendency of nearly all its inhabitants to feel alike and act
together in moments of supreme crisis.

George Orwell, *The Lion and the Unicorn:*
Socialism and the English Genius
(London, 1941), 33

THE FALLING-OUT

Back in the School once again, Ashby divided his time between research and
fitting out the new building on slender finances. In the aftermath of the First
World War, British society had new expectations, but the country's economy was
plainly not up to meeting them. Public funding of higher education until the inter-
war period had been very restricted in comparison with France and, especially,
Germany.[1] This was particularly conspicuous in the humanities. The British
Academy, founded in 1901 to promote research in the humanities, was unable to
procure any public funding until the ex-Prime Minister, Lord Balfour, was made
its President in 1923. He obtained £2,000 in 1924, a figure which was sustained
until 1932 when it dropped to £1,800.[2] The plight of the British School at
Rome, in short, was the norm for a nation which had other priorities.

The cost of heating Lutyens's building was Ashby's most pressing
problem. Fuel and light rose from £91 in 1919–20 (about 3.3% of the School's
expenditure) to £535 two years later, representing nearly 17% of the School's
expenditure.[3] Dozens of letters passed between Evelyn Shaw, as the School's
London Secretary, and Ashby on this account. Ashby complained bitterly that the
west-facing wing on the ground floor (that is the library and his quarters) was
cold and damp. The building works also began again. A new common-room was
needed. During these years two of the artists' studios at the back were employed
as a refectory/common-room. There were also more scholars to consider now.
There is no reason to doubt that Ashby was an assiduous, if idiosyncratic,
administrator. After all, he succeeded in getting the British School built and
working, almost despite the architects and engineers. But, as he bridged this
challenge, and as 1920 passed into 1921, Ashby's life took a new direction.

FIG. 28. Dr and Mrs Ashby at the British School at Rome, *c.* 1924.
(British School at Rome Archive Neg. No. TA LVIII,30)

Sometime after returning from his excavations in Malta in the spring of 1921 he began to court (Caroline) May Price-Williams, a cousin of Walter Ashburner, an old friend and director of the British Institute at Florence (a Subscriber to the School since its foundation in 1901). Within weeks, improbable as it seems, Ashby proposed and married (Fig. 28).

May Ashby remains virtually unknown to us. She had been working in the library under Eugénie Strong's direction when the courtship began. Was she an expatriate, or simply visiting her relatives in Italy? Small, round-faced, and a little younger than Ashby, May has been cast in the role of scapegoat for Ashby's ultimate fate. The photographs also reveal that she aged quickly over the following decade, her greying hair soon matching Ashby's.

Ashby's letter to Evelyn Shaw of 1 July 1921, describing his forthcoming betrothal, foresaw the circumstances:

> Dear Shaw,
> I sent a confidential note to Smith from Sicily ... as to Mrs Strong's nervous condition ... The last development is my engagement to Miss May Price-Williams, a cousin of Walter Ashburner of Florence ... and we hope to be married quietly there soon and spend the summer here. Mrs S. has been a good deal better than she was in the spring — to me at any rate — but she obviously wants a rest and change and what I found difficult before is likely to be a great deal more so to my wife, who would naturally occupy the position of lady of the house. Mrs Strong says she would willingly give that up, but I do not think she would really be able to do so. Besides, her nervous condition and her dominating character, which I have always found, as I think you realize, very hard to bear, are now really unendurable to me. I have given in to her for the sake of peace and quietude for more than I ought, but now I cannot do it ...
> I do not feel either that I could expose my wife (who has worked with her in the library) to such an atmosphere of unrest as she creates nor to the bad temper and nerves from which various people have suffered, among them my mother to whom she did behave very unkindly last summer. Her own sister too who was here this spring had an awful time with her.
> ... As to myself, I would say that my fiancée is not very far from my own age, so that I anticipate no children, and we should be prepared to live in the rooms I at present occupy ...
> I hope this letter will not seem heartless and inconsiderate. I have said a good deal of it to Mrs Strong, but very unwillingly — but I felt I ought not to go behind her back.
> Yours very sincerely,
> Thomas Ashby.

Ashby harboured no secret fear of Eugénie Strong. He understood her implicitly. Hence he was attempting to have her out-housed. At first Eugénie Strong agreed to the proposal. But within a week Ashby was writing again to Shaw to say that she had turned against the notion. By the 7 July Ashby was confiding that a letter from May Price-Williams to Eugénie Strong had been received badly. Ashby was anxious lest the Committee draw the wrong conclusions: 'I should like them to know that she [May Price-Williams] replied to it in a most friendly tone'. Shaw replied quickly (on 11 July): 'Do not worry any more about this affair. I do not know why so much fuss has been made about it'.

Eugénie Strong left for London before Ashby's wedding in mid-July. But the die was cast. She resented the intrusion of new blood into her domain. More galling still was the fact that May was not an academic, simply a middle-class woman who offered Ashby companionship. The first major confrontation had its origins before Eugénie Strong's return. The Ashbys decided to keep guard dogs in the School. Ashby had always been fond of dogs, as his many photographs of them illustrate. But these dogs met swift disapproval. On the 16 September he noted that he would erect wire netting between the front door and the students' door in order to protect them from the dogs. By November Eugénie Strong had evidently written to Shaw, who replied (10 November) urging Ashby to 'arrange to keep your own private dogs in the School and do away with those ferocious animals. For some time I have been nervous about these and Lord Esher is horrified at having to keep the brutes. Why not have your own terrier?'. Ashby pleaded (on 16 November) that the dogs were School dogs; he had no intention of keeping his own dogs. Shaw replied eleven days later: 'we are very nervous here lest the brutes should devour one of the students or staff'. By late November the Ashbys had embarked upon a search for a terrier. So began the story that May Ashby was fond of dogs.

Evelyn Shaw was soon completely embroiled in the School's internal tribulations. A letter to Rennell Rodd dated 31 October 1922 — fifteen months after Ashby's betrothal — sets out his view of the situation:

> As regards the Ashby business the proceedings were a little less happy. They all recognize what a hopeless creature Mrs. Ashby is. Ashby himself is in such a state of anxiety about his personal relations with Mrs. Strong that I feared he would resign, and this I knew would lead to a clean sweep of the lot, much to the gratification of all the other faculties. But we managed to soothe him.
>
> In the course of three solid hours I learnt enough to know that the Faculty look upon his lot as not a happy one placed as he is between a stupid wife and a domineering Assistant.

The struggle for supremacy, however, became increasingly more substantive. First, despite a directive by Shaw to the contrary, May Ashby took to running the burgeoning household of servants. After this there was the question of accommodation. A confrontation soon occurred. The issue boiled down to the allocation of two bedrooms. Who should have the warmer bedrooms on the first floor? The dispute began in 1923 when Ashby expressed a wish that his wife and he might have separate bedrooms. By March 1924, Ashby and Eugénie Strong were locked into a silent, though furious, feud about the matter. When the Executive Committee met in early March, it was decided to despatch Arthur Smith, the chairman of the Faculty of Archaeology, History and Letters, to Rome, to arbitrate. His report, dated 8 April 1924, illustrates how every conceivable detail of the School was studiously examined by the grandees on the Executive Committee:[4]

> *Memorandum for the Executive Sub-Committee*
> I reached Rome on March 17th, with the discussion of the Executive Sub-Committee fresh in my mind, and I carefully examined the question of the assignment of rooms, on the spot.
> The differences of view seemed irreconcilable. A suggestion I threw out, that a joint conference might find an agreed solution, was not acceptable, and the only thing to be done was to study the two apartments in detail, in company with the respective occupants.
> If two additional rooms are available, there is a prima facie fairness in giving one to each officer. But in approaching the question I feel firstly, that the fact that the plans showed a room as assigned to the Assistant Director which was, on further consideration, given to the Director, cannot be said to create a vested interest in the room. Secondly, I do not think that the matter need be considered on the basis of parity of treatment. The real question to be considered is what division of the apartments is most conducive to the general comfort of the two officers, *assuming* that the additional rooms are used for that purpose.
> [SKETCH]
> Mrs Strong at present has Bedroom, Study and Library, and Sitting-Room. The Sitting-Room serves the combined purposes of Drawing-Room and Dining-Room, but the Study can be used on occasion as a second sitting-room. The points emphasised by Mrs Strong were that she would like to have room for a piano, to have room for preparations and service in connection with a tea-party, and to have space for occasional ironing, and other similar domestic operations.
> These are all desirable amenities, but on the whole it appeared to me that even in their absence Mrs Strong was the enviable occupant of a very charming apartment.
> [SKETCHES]
> Dr. Ashby at present has:-
> *Ground Floor*: Combined Office and Library, Sitting Room;
> *Upper Floor*: Two Bedrooms
> The Office-Library is full, not to say over-full, of books and papers, and not capable of use except as an office and study.
> The Sitting-Room serves the combined purposes of Drawing-Room and Dining-room. In addition the room has large bookcases with a somewhat ragged overflow of the Library. I pointed out to the Director that a collector must accept the incidental discomforts of his pursuits, but he replied, with undeniable force, that his library was strictly germane to the purposes of the School: that it was available as a supplement to the School Library, with a corresponding catalogue, and that consequently there was no sitting-room in the apartment that could be considered private.
> Upstairs are the two bedrooms, at present forming part of the apartment, and of which one is proposed to be withdrawn.

Leaving on one side the fact that Dr. and Mrs Ashby are agreed in refusing to share a room, the question to be settled is whether what is offered is reasonable accommodation. Dr. Ashby was decidedly of opinion that a ground-floor bedroom was inadmissable [sic] on account of damp, combined with sunlessness in winter — a point of which I was not in a position to judge. He also considered the upper room too small for joint occupation. It is about 14 feet each way, and is as large as many double rooms in a London flat, or a Roman hotel, but I think it is true that it would be inconveniently small for permanent double use in the climate of Rome. There are also manifest discomforts attaching to the suggested use of the ground floor room as a dressing room. It is only connected by a general stair with bedrooms, bath-room, etc.

It appears to me that to refuse the use of the second upstairs room is to gravely diminish the amenities attaching to the apartment of a married Director.

As to the two downstairs rooms, I feel that the Director is entitled to one of them in the absence of any private sitting-room. The second one did not seem to me to be applicable conveniently at present to any School purpose, and might therefore be assigned also to the Director.

I was, however, much impressed by the fact that the Library accommodation will be exhausted before long, and that there are no readily available means of extending it. If, therefore, the subject is thought to be open to reconsideration on the lines I have suggested, I would propose that, in giving the two rooms to the Director, the Committee should warn him that the whole question must come up for review, in connexion with the needs of the Library, at a not distant date, — say, in 1927.
[Signed] A.H. Smith

Within days of Smith's departure, Eugénie Strong, conscious of her duty to the School and her perceived friendship with Shaw, withdrew her claim to the extra bedroom. She requested a maid's room elsewhere in its stead. She also proposed numerous alterations. Nevertheless, she could not resist reminding the committee of how fortunate the Ashbys were. By 7 May she had compromised to the extent of asking Shaw 'for a piece of garden — 4 m. square outside ... for planting roses'. Eugénie Strong must have anticipated the outcome in this trivial battle. She was well aware of the School's financial plight. The Faculty of Archaeology, History and Letters at face value could not maintain her salary. The poorly finished building, too, needed a large number of domestic staff that, together with the heating bills, was draining the fledgling School of its slender resources. Shaw wrote on 12 June telling her that officially May Ashby had no authority whatsoever in the administration of the School. He knew from the Executive Committee meeting of 30 May that the decision had been made to terminate Eugénie Strong's contract, but that it needed ratifying by the Faculty. She misjudged Shaw's motives. His mandarin tone elicited a chastened response

FIG. 29. Thomas and May Ashby. *(British School at Rome Archive 147)*

from her, in a rambling letter dated 17 June. Placing her complete trust in the School Secretary, she attempted to assess her relationship with the Ashbys (Fig. 29):

> Mrs A belongs to a class who get their way in the end by sheer persistence. Her husband whether through love or fear of her always gives in — there's an end of it. After all none of us can be rude to the Director's wife ... I however am in a peculiarly difficult and often painful position. Not in the least because I am Asst. Director, but because I am primarily attached to Ashby, to whom I am bound by many ties of common work and interests, and I hate to appear to criticize him. And I by no means dislike his wife — far from it — only they are both colosaly [sic] selfish not from temperament so much as from circumstances. She because after provincial and colonial life, she is determined to have *comfort* and a *home* at any cost (it's this that she cares for more than 'society') ... and he because up to the time of his marriage, he lived entirely in the shelter of his mother's petticoats. As a friend (of his!) wittily said: 'the old lady knew how to run the School for the benefit of her son — and he tries to run it for the benefit of his wife'. As another amusing Italo-British friend said — he is not amorous, he is uxorious. Fortunately it does not harm the students he is very good there.

She ended by once more returning to old themes: designated
responsibilities and space, not least to plant some roses. She expressed anxiety
for May Ashby: 'she looks so ill and so worried. In a sense I am convinced she
wishes to help her husband — perhaps all of us — I had a very friendly talk with
her on Sunday and tried to persuade her that no official residence in the world —
not even Downing Street — was worth worrying over as she was over this place'.

But the Executive Committee had long since lost patience. On the 30 May
1924 they had met to consider the renewal of Ashby's and Eugénie Strong's
contracts: those present were the Earl of Crawford and Balcarres (Chairman), Sir
Rennell Rodd, Arthur Smith (representing the Faculty of Archaeology), Sir
Reginald Blomfield (Faculty of Architecture), Sir David Cameron (the Faculties
of Printing and Engraving), Sir George Frampton (Faculty of Sculpture) and
Evelyn Shaw.[5]

Mr Smith explained:

> Everyone is aware of the constant friction between the Directors —
> only persons who have been in close contact with affairs at the School
> — like Mr Shaw — can realise how this has permeated all departments
> of the School and added to difficulties. When the question of the re-
> appointment was approached the Faculty looked about for some
> remedy. Everything was considered. We found that we were getting
> Mrs Strong 'vested' in us. Mrs Strong's main appointment is the care
> of the library. From the first she has done work which is highly
> appreciated by the Faculty and the Embassy — and good work for the
> School. But at the same time we cannot afford the salary of a person
> who is not doing the work of the librarian. We don't feel that the
> library will ever be in order — with Mrs Strong who is no longer
> young. We feel it our duty towards our trustees and subscribers to
> make a new arrangement. The state of affairs has been going on from
> year to year.

The debate continued; the chairman asked Sir David Cameron to offer an
opinion: 'It does not appear to have any effect upon the working of the students
… Mrs Strong is the only one as far as I know to take any pains with them — Dr.
Ashby does not seem to — it is true he takes them out — She struck me as being
popular … the centre of the School'.

Each member then added comments about Eugénie Strong (above, Fig. 21).
Sir Rennell Rodd, a lifelong friend of Eugénie Strong, proved the most trenchant
in his views:

> When we talk about the social side we attach too much importance to
> Mrs Strong — when she has come to us [referring to Rome Embassy]
> she has asked us to invite students to our houses and to help relieve
> them from the daily routine. That is the utmost she can be charged
> with except when she lectures — she gives these lectures to a number
> of important people and that does the School good — it gets us talked

about ... I have watched the whole thing from the beginning. Confidentially I may say that my opinion of Ashby is that he is an overgrown schoolboy — he talks like a schoolboy — there isn't a spark of inspiration in him — Nor does he get any credit for us in other schools in Rome — he has no push — no inspiration. If we lose Mrs Strong we lose terribly ... They are both great friends of mine and I try to look at the question unprejudiced.

The discussion rambled. Mr Smith interjected at one point: 'The Faculty of Archaeology do not attach over great importance to Dr. Ashby's topography'. Discussion continued:

Lord Crawford: 'You suggest we should invite the Fac[ulty] of Arch[aeolo]gy to reconsider, but we have no status ...'
Mr Smith: 'I would suggest we adopt the method mentioned at the meeting of the EX[ecutive] Cttee the other day — it was I think Lord Esher's suggestion that we should send the directors notices now, appointing them for another year and say the appointments are under consideration as regarding continuing ...'
Lord Crawford: '... if they both leave will Faculty put both salaries together and let us appoint men of great distinction'.

Shaw swiftly expedited the matter. On the 20 June 1924 the Faculty of Archaeology, History and Letters agreed to support the Executive Committee, adding that they wished to be involved in selecting Thomas Ashby's successor.[6] Meeting the following day, the Executive Committee decided to enact Smith's proposal. Bernard Ashmole recounted that:[7]

In the summer of 1924 we had a surprise visit from John Forsdyke, Secretary of the Archaeological Faculty of the British School at Rome. He explained that, owing to persistent quarrelling between Dr Ashby, the Director, his newly-married wife, and Mrs Arthur Strong, the Assistant Director, the Managing Committee had decided to dismiss both of them and that the post of Director would therefore be vacant. Would I like to consider accepting it?

Ashmole was then aged 30. The end of the Ashby era was at hand.

Ashby accepted the matter with fortitude; Eugénie Strong was no less stoic. Twelve years later, though, on the occasion of the proposed closure of the School as a result of sanctions imposed by Britain on Italy during the Abyssinian crisis, Eugénie Strong, in a letter to Shaw, reached a conclusion that, with hindsight, was all too apparent: 'You must get more money out of your Trustees, or B.S.R., for no fault of its Directors, will continue to go downhill ... If members of the Committee came out more often they would realise how multiple are now the interests which have to be watched in Rome'.[8]

In fact the Executive Committee itself was broaching this latter point as early as the autumn of 1924. For after reaching its conclusion in the spring about removing Ashby and Eugénie Strong, a moment of doubt arose. On 11 October Reginald Blomfield wrote a long letter to Evelyn Shaw which was copied to Lord Esher:

My dear Shaw,
    I have visited the School at Rome ... Ashby and Mrs Strong appear to be on excellent terms, united by the bonds of affliction! ... I do not feel happy about the change of Direction, & fear it may be difficult for the new man. It is too late now to change, but there are one or two points which I would ask you to bring before the Council.
    1) I fear the late Heads have been harshly treated. It is a serious matter for both of them, & particularly for Ashby, to lose their job; and I did not realize till I came here how much they have both done for the School. I learn that they have both made considerable donations to the School from their own libraries & their own resources; & I gather that little or no acknowledgement of this has been made by the authorities responsible. I wish our attention had been called to this last July.
    2) Personally, I was opposed to the change, but I understand that the Art side had no *locus standi* in the matter, the decision resting entirely with the Faculty of Archaeology ... I think the time has come to re-organize the Executive so that the control shall be in the hands of one body, viz. a Council representing all the Faculties, in which the Faculty of Archaeology would have its place side by side with the Faculties of the Arts, with neither less power, nor more.
    ... Since writing this I have seen the Ambassador, and discussed the position with him. He told me that he had not been consulted at all in regard to the change, to which I said that having Sir Rennell Rodd, the Council did not want to trouble him. All the same it would have been better to have had his opinion, & it would have been undoubtedly opposed to the change. The fact is, the whole thing was rushed.
    The Ambassador told me that he feared the change was not to the interest of the School in that the Italians would not welcome the change of Ashby & Mrs Strong, both of whom they like and believe in, for a young & relatively inexperienced man ...
    I write frankly because I am sincerely anxious for the permanent success of the School. Please show this letter to the Chairman & bring it up before the Executive.
Yours sincerely,
Reginald Blomfield

Wearily, on 24 October, Shaw replied:

Dear Blomfield,
    I am personally sorry that I have not had the opportunity of refreshing your memory as to the history of the negotiations before circulating your letter.
Yours sincerely,
Evelyn Shaw

Blomfield's circulated letter to the Executive drew short replies, except from Arthur Smith, the Chairman of the Faculty of Archaeology. He pointed out that the gifts made by Ashby and Eugénie Strong were recognized in the Annual Reports of the Faculty. He declined responsibility for initiating 'the matter of terminating Dr. Ashby's engagement', and blamed the arts faculties which bemoaned the fact that he did not provide sufficient guidance to their students. Smith then pursued all Blomfield's detailed points, correcting them as he saw it. Rennell Rodd was rather more cavalier in his reply to Shaw on 25 October:

> Between ourselves I always felt that those old gentlemen in 1 Bloomsbury Square looked at things rather from the clerk of the catalogues' point of view, who as Whistler said 'files the 15th Century and pigeon holes the antique', and did not quite realise that the telescope has a big as well as a small end, and they were looking through the wrong one. But what is done is done ... Blomfield is right in a general way, but there are obstacles which he does not understand or wish to understand.

Within a month, however, Shaw was able to report that Blomfield's views were in a minority. Rennell Rodd hurried from Naples to Rome and on 8 November 1924 he reported to Shaw that:

> ... almost everyone I meet deplores the decision, because other things apart our School was the only one which could compete in any way with the German Institute with its great library. In spite of Ashby's eccentricities he had the regard of all the Italian archaeologists and they are all very much upset at his going. In his own particular line he is considered one of the greatest authorities and his collections and maps which have been at the disposal of students are almost unique in their way. Between ourselves I have been told that a member of the Archaeological Faculty repudiated any responsibility for the decision which he said was taken by the Executive Board. If this really was said it was one of the half truths which are worse than whole lies.

Shaw copied Rodd's letter to Lord Esher. Esher was angry; he annotated Shaw's covering letter, writing (11/13 November): 'He [Rodd] was one of the persons responsible for the changes. How can he escape it?'. Rodd repeated his sad thesis on reaching his London home in Cavendish Square on 22 November. Shaw set about quelling the uprising. He prepared detailed briefing papers for the Executive Committee on Thursday 4 December. Blomfield's points were dealt with clinically, followed by a summary of the charter to illustrate the constitutional motives for the decision taken in June. Inevitably, Shaw shepherded the Committee through the impasse of their own making.

The Times on the 21 January 1925 recounted the 'coming changes' to the British School at Rome. The 'State of Finances' was set roundly before the annual meeting of the Faculty of Archaeology, History and Letters held the previous day. 'The financial position cannot be described as good', Arthur Smith told the audience, which meant that the appointment of the Assistant Director could no longer be renewed. A lecture followed by Mr Bernard Ashmole, who, Smith admitted in summing up the evening, had been appointed to reorganize the School with the retirement in the course of the next summer of Thomas Ashby. Ashmole at that point in time had published three short notes and two book reviews.[9] Whatever Ashmole's promise, his appointment cannot have impressed Ashby or his peers in Rome.

That spring Sir George Clausen visited Rome and made a sympathetic sketch of Ashby, later included in the Foreword to Ashby's *Aqueducts*, and an austere oil-painting showing him in profile as if he were a Gonzaga of Mantua. David Evans, a sculpture scholar, prepared a bronze bust of Ashby at the same time, casting it in 1926.[10] The painter and ex-Scholar Winifred Knights, then married to the scholar–painter Tom Monnington, recorded that it was a sad time at the School (Fig. 30).[11] Eugénie Strong, now aged 65, departed for London, where the King awarded her the CBE and a dinner was given in her honour by her

FIG. 30. Drawing of Thomas Ashby by Winifred Knights, *c.* 1922.
(Collection: Author)

pupils and friends. Afterwards, she returned to Rome, to a spacious flat in the Via Balbo.[12] Ashby, by contrast, left for the meeting of the British Association for the Advancement of Science, where he was President of the anthropological section, and spoke about aqueducts. The School's first phase was over, and a second, less noteworthy, era was about to begin.

Reflecting on the crisis that afflicted the School, Bruno Bonelli, an administrator appointed by Eugénie Strong in 1921, found it all very sad. Ashby was a great man in the eyes of the School's staff; his wife was a nobody. Bonelli went so far as to describe May Ashby as a witch.[13] Many of the staff believed that someone had manipulated the whole affair deliberately to get rid of Ashby and Strong.

Bernard Ashmole arrived in the autumn of 1925. 'It was an extraordinarily awkward situation', he recalled, 'because both Dr Ashby and Mrs Strong were still living in Rome and there was naturally a good deal of sympathy with them'.[14] There were numerous problems in the School, food first of all. When the tea ran out, old pots were simply filled up with water. Everyone was rationed, or rather given an entitlement. Eventually Ashmole sacked the cook and hired a new one, a Russian who had been Conductor of the Band on the Tsar's yacht.

The Ashmoles were warmly regarded, I believe, by the School's staff. By 1927 the circumstances had been stabilized to the extent that Evelyn Shaw ventured a personal, handwritten, letter, written at home, in a reflective mood that is so different from his correspondence with either Ashby or Strong:

> 20.2.27
> My dear Ashmole,
>
> I hope that [Augustus] John turned up without his harem ...
>
> Blomfield who made such an ass of himself when the old regime was abolished tackled me the other day about the unbearable behaviour of Mrs. Strong towards you and the School in general. He had heard from some friend lately in Rome that Mrs. S. was still at her games and he thinks it is high time something were done to counteract the ... gossip and influence of the woman.
>
> He suspects that Esher should take the matter up through the F.O. and now privately admits that the School was put back 10 years by the selfish conduct and incompetence of the woman.
>
> It is unpleasant to think that the damned woman cannot be bridled, but it is a great thing to know that here at home there is none left of the old school who does not wish you well.
>
> In fact they all realise at last what a blessing you are to them and what a mercy it is for the school to be quit of all humbuggery.
>
> ... I have never had such a peaceful time or carefree mind in regard to the School as during the last year or so. The absence of bickering and complaints on the part of students etc. is a ... delightful experience. The feeling that all goes well ...
>
> Therefore think a little more about yourself and take things more

easily … I should like to receive a letter from Mrs Ashmole telling me
that *you* are behaving as you should.
Bless you.
Yours
Evelyn Shaw
Rodd will be seeing you. I shall write and amuse him about
Blomfield's repentance.

FINAL YEARS

The Ashbys first moved to an apartment in Viale Mazzini, and then to one in a
sizeable house in a new development near the Borghese Gardens in the Via
Vincenzo Bellini, a short distance from the British School. Ralegh Radford
recalled that the latter was a 'squalid flat'. Possibly it just seemed strange to the
young Radford to encounter the legendary Ashby in modest surroundings after
the ample grandeur of the British School.[15] In reality, as Ashby had inhabited
hotels for much of his life, it is doubtful that the circumstances of his new home
bothered him. He made no effort, as far as we know, to find any other position.
Instead, it seems that the Ashbys lived off their modest private income,
supplemented by royalties and fees for writing.

In the spring of 1926 he embarked upon a continent-wide tour of the
United States of America, lecturing for the Archaeological Institute of America.
Sketches for letters, presumably then typed and sent to his wife, survive in the
School's archive. The trip included a sea-voyage from New York to Panama. His
letters are highly descriptive — the work of a practised topographer with an
interest in anthropology. In California he jotted down that 'the prosperity is
positively appalling; the centres of the cities are hideous (the centre more like
hell than anything else) and then you pass into lovely residential quarters'. Of the
coast at Santa Monica, he commented upon the flowers though preferred the
'wild beauty of S. Devon cliffs'. As a seasoned traveller, Ashby took advantage
of every opportunity, and even saw many movies.

The inexorable drive did not dwindle — quite the contrary. Ashby had kept
up a steady stream of publications since returning from the Isonzo front. His
study of the Via Flaminia, written with Fell, his Ambulance Unit colleague,
appeared in the *Journal of Roman Studies* in 1921. The next in this series, on the
Via Tiberina, was published in 1924. In his last year at the School, he published
Turner's Visions of Rome with Halton and Truscott Smith Ltd of London.
Although little more than an illustrated essay, it formed part of an *oeuvre* which
in the early '20s included short studies of Lievin Cruyl, Canaletto and, a little
later, the eighteenth-century collector, Lord Bristol. But as his Directorship
neared its end, he once again began to concentrate upon his book about the
aqueducts of ancient Rome. In 1925, as we have seen, he delivered a lecture to
the British Association for the Advancement of Science about his interim
thoughts on the subject. As he struggled with this great work, the exigencies of

earning an income intervened. Hence, he devoted much of his first year after leaving the Directorship to writing *The Roman Campagna in Classical Times*, which was published by Benn the following year. This was a synthesis of his previous studies for the general reader. Without doubt it is his best-known book. John Ward-Perkins described it as follows:[16]

> [It] is not a guide book; nor is it a literary classic like George Dennis's *Cities and Cemeteries of the Etruscans*. It is the deeply felt historical interpretation of a countryside, made under conditions which are now themselves a matter of history. Other books have been, and no doubt will continue to be, written about parts of the Campagna. But nothing can replace Ashby's work.

Ashby's young disciple, Giuseppe Lugli, by this time his constant walking companion, commented that it did not read like a novel: 'Rarely Ashby allowed himself lyrical effects, poetic phrases, these were not in his character; he was the surgeon making neat cuts, using a minimal number of adjectives that lead immediately to the essential part of the matter'.[17]

In 1927, in collaboration with Lugli, he spent the summer at Poggio Mirteto preparing a volume of the *Forma Italia*.[18] Lugli recounted in his affectionate memoir how they combed the Sabina (Fig. 31). Although this volume was never completed, clearly Ashby's fascination for the Campagna Romana remained insatiable.

In these years, besides writing articles on Rome for magazines and the *Encyclopedia Britannica*, he prepared a revised edition of *The Architecture of Ancient Rome* (1927) that forms the second volume of Anderson and Spiers's *Architecture of Greece and Rome*. Ashby made an extensive revision of this Batsford handbook which had first appeared in 1902. He wrote, as he stated in the preface, as an archaeologist testing theories which he hoped would interest the architectural profession. He titled himself 'the late Director of the British School at Rome', and remarked that the 'enlarged British School at Rome offers facilities to students of Architecture to come and study the original monuments on the spot'.[19] Following this substantial editorial task, he committed two years to the revision of Samuel B. Platner's *A Topographical Dictionary of Rome* (1929). This endeavour, it soon became clear to Ashby, was far greater than he had envisaged initially. Platner's first edition had been published in 1912 to some critical acclaim. He had invited Ashby to collaborate on a revision before the First World War intervened. Following this enforced interruption, Platner sailed for Europe in August 1921. On the voyage he was overtaken by a serious illness and within 24 hours he was dead. Platner's widow asked Ashby to complete the book. Ashby estimated that *circa* 20 to 25 per cent of the final version was written by him. He not only wrote about aqueducts, gates and roads, but also articles on the Forum and Palatine that Platner had failed to complete. The result

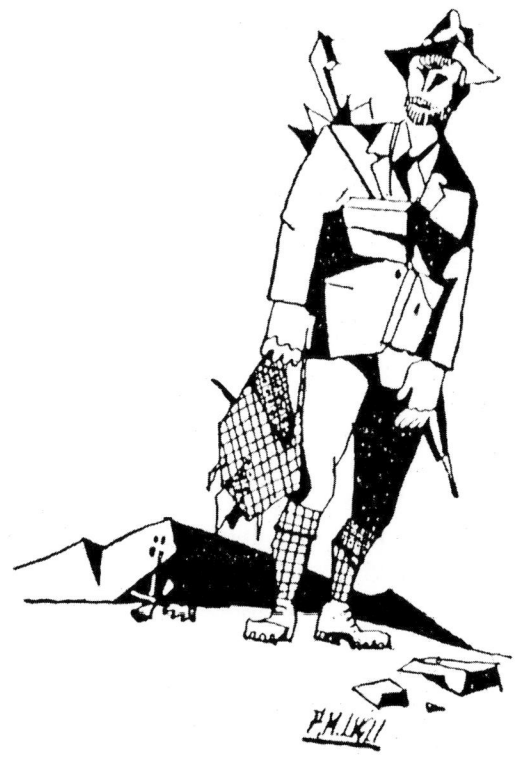

Fig. 31. Sketch of Ashby by Giuseppe Lugli.
(British School at Rome Archive)

was deemed a classic, and even today it is perhaps the most consulted index for the topography of ancient Rome. Following this Ashby wrote *Some Italian Scenes and Festivals* (1929) — a book that he dedicated to his wife and that made use of a lifetime of travels and photographs. Sections of the book grew out of his fascination for traditional costumes, then still to be seen regularly at festivals in the Abruzzo and on Sardinia. Cautiously he welcomed the fact that the 'Socialist wave has passed by, and the present Government is certainly not unfriendly to the national church ... [encouraging] these village festivals so dear to her people'.[20] The book covers familiar territory. Three chapters concern the Campagna Romana; then there are chapters on festivals in the Abruzzo, in north Latium and on Sardinia. Like *The Roman Campagna in Classical Times*, the style is unmistakably that of a Victorian scholar writing for an interested lay audience.

After these books Ashby's health began to suffer. Precisely what happened is not known. A letter to Ashby from Mrs Platner, once in the School's archive, is more revealing. Ashby, noted his correspondent, had:[21]

> ... been in an English hospital for some time ... No doubt you have
> been working too hard — it is easy to overdo these days, especially in
> certain lines of work. I hope yours is not a nervous breakdown — that
> is what happened to one of my dear sisters and it is evidently going to
> be a long hard pull up hill again.

His eyesight had deteriorated badly. Did this trigger preoccupations about finding
an income? Was he overcome at last by his treatment by the British School? Or had
he simply invested too much of himself in this series of books? In search of a rest
he took a voyage to Australia, repeating the successful tour he had made before the
war. Following this, perhaps heeding the encouragement of his friends and wife, he
finally threw his energies into *The Aqueducts of Ancient Rome* (Figs 32 and 33).
Yet, even now, he continued to update his earlier articles, jotting down new
references and thoughts in the margins of the *Papers of the British School at Rome*
6 (1913), on subjects as diverse as Thomas Jenkins and Malta.[22]

The Ashbys in these years largely disappeared from British view. Neither
Ashby nor Strong, as far as we know, accepted the Fellowships of the British
School offered in their dismissal letters. Ashby never visited the School, as far as
Bruno Bonelli could recall. Instead, he became associated with the British

FIG. 32. The Aqua Claudia in the section between the Orti Variani and Porta Maggiore
incorporated into the Aurelian Walls, *c.* 1894. *(British School at Rome Archive
Neg. No. 216 (GFN F 202))*

FIG. 33. The Aqua Claudia in the Via di San Gregorio, *c.* 1903. *(British School at Rome Archive Neg. No. VI,44 (GFN F 2055))*

Academy of Arts in Rome on Via Margutta, being elected secretary in 1929.[23] Nevertheless, he was not forgotten in Britain. In 1927 he was elected a Fellow of the British Academy, and three years later Christ Church appointed him a Senior Research Fellow. He had effectively quit British academic life, choosing instead, in his inimitable way of following his father, to retire early. Arthur Smith, in his memoir for the British Academy, appears to have lost touch with him after 1925, even though he himself was Director of the School between 1928 and 1930. Only Ian Richmond, elected Director in 1930, maintained a friendship with the Ashbys. Thomas and May had become expatriates, following the Victorian and Edwardian pattern. British attitudes to Ashby almost certainly puzzled his Italian colleagues, which may account for Francesco Tomassetti's long essay about him in the series entitled 'Scrittori contemporanei di cose romane', published in the *Archivio della Reale Società Romana di Storia Patria* (1927). Tomassetti introduced Ashby as:[24]

> Roman by his long residence and for his love of our city and towards its grand past ... we are happy to have this opportunity to pay homage to our distinguished and illustrious colleague, in the circumstances of leaving the direction of the British School at Rome, an important office undertaken in a dignified and proper manner for the not brief period of twenty years.

For a scholar in his early fifties, Tomassetti was paying Ashby a notable honour; Rodolfo Lanciani was yet to be lauded in this way.

Italy, however, was changing. The rise of Fascism must have impinged upon Ashby's liberal mind. In these years Mussolini's projects cultivated 'all things Roman, Roman of the Caesars, heirs of Empire and world power'.[25] Many of Ashby's friends were seduced by the opportunities offered by the new regime, as new plans were made for exhibiting Rome's past. At the same time, new suburbs were being built around the British School — outward expressions of Italy's increasing prosperity. Other manifestations began to trouble him: the battle for grain, as Mussolini described it, led to the increasing cultivation of the Campagna. Yet, it seems likely that Ashby, scion of Quaker family, subscribed to the philosophy of his mentor, Francis Haverfield: 'I have a great dislike to mixing up politics with learning' (see Chapter Two).[26] His opinions are more trenchantly expressed in a memo of June 1924. Here he lamented that the foreign Schools had not been permitted to help as Rome quadrupled in size and that innumerable discoveries in the building operations were recorded poorly:[27]

> Valuable information of all kinds has been irretrievably lost owing to this short sighted policy of not inviting foreign cooperation in funds and supervision. The old saying that Italy belongs to humanity comes of course into conflict with Italian national sentiment, and has in the case of a young and sensitive nation probably led to some excess in the other direction … Of course I know there is no danger of my Italian colleagues becoming acquainted with my views, or otherwise I should be drowned in one of the volcanic lakes for which this part of Italy is so well known.

This new Augustan age, by contrast, suited Eugénie Strong. She developed her salon in the Via Balbo. To her flat came a stream of visitors in search of advice or company. One man's impression of his hostess was as follows:[28]

> Her manners, like her outlook, were aristocratic, or even imperious, and her movements, which she limited to the minimum because of arthritis, were self-conscious and studied, but not only for the economy of effort. I once heard her describe the sanctity of demeanour which made the celebration of Mass by Leo XIII so memorable, and immediately and ever since I realised how completely Mrs Strong's own impressive presence outwardly embodied her immense learning, her intuition and her realisation of her own exceptional gifts, combined with a fundamental and less easily recognised humility. Her appearance was the most vivid possible expression of her personality.

How much Ashby saw of Eugénie Strong after 1925 is not known. In an article read to the Congress of Roman Studies in Rome in April 1928 and published in May, she reminded her audience of Ashby's great contribution to the British School and included Clausen's sketch in the publication.[29] Richard Krautheimer accompanied them both up Trajan's Column in 1928, when he observed their old relationship to be unchanged, Eugénie Strong being the dominant member of the couple.[30]

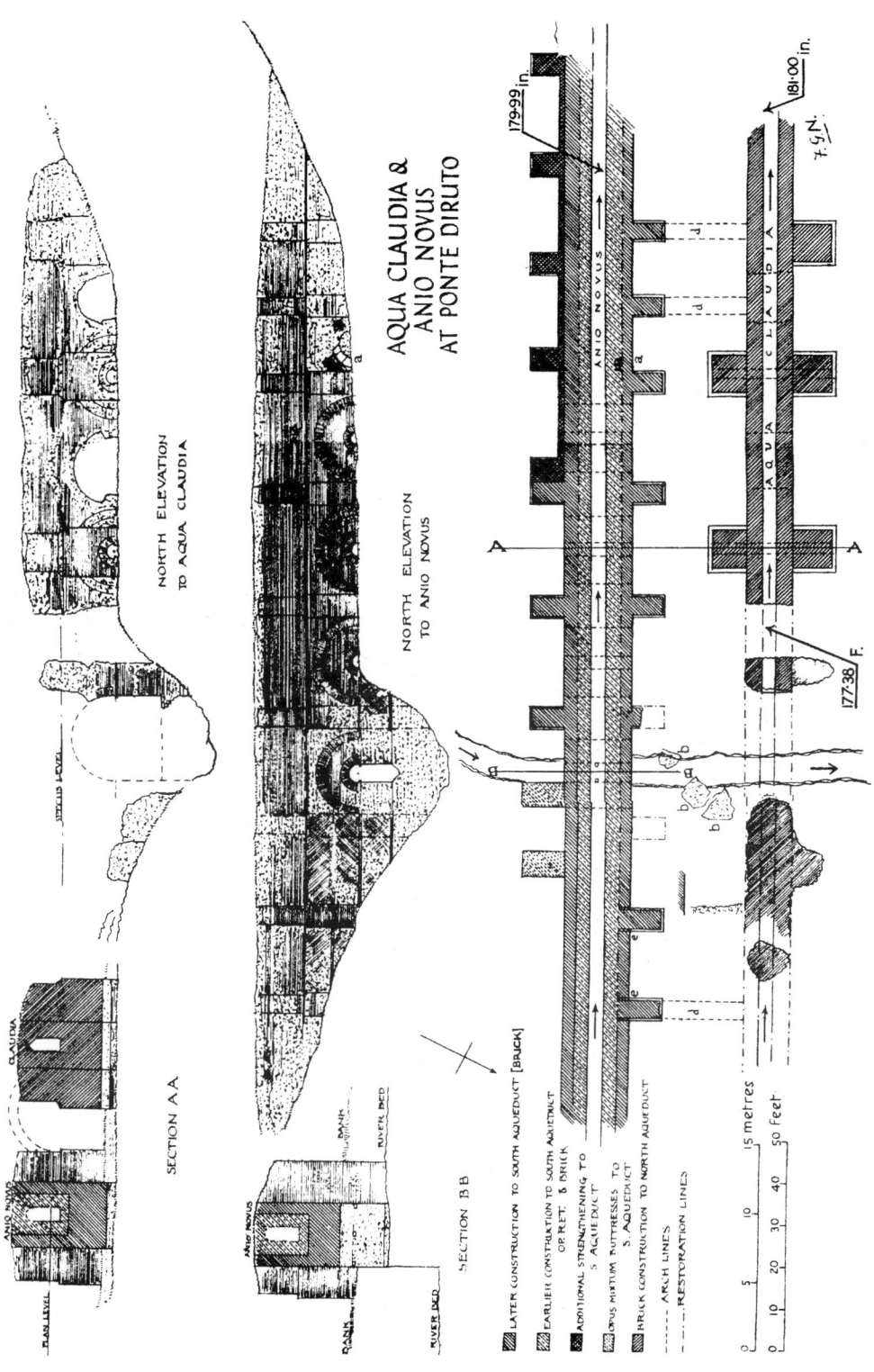

FIG. 34. Sections and plans of the Aqua Claudia and the Anio Novus at Ponte Diruto. *(From Ashby, Aqueducts, opposite p. 216)*

The death of Rodolfo Lanciani on 21 May 1929 robbed Ashby of his last great mentor, and provided him with the occasion to write a long appreciation of the 'maestro' in the *Archivio della Reale Società Romana di Storia Patria*.[31] It was to his memory that Ashby dedicated *Aqueducts*. Ian Richmond, who saw *Aqueducts* through the press, remarked that the closing words of the preface of this book, in which Ashby remembered his debt to Lanciani, 'will read with a certain pathos: but they have been retained, implementing his wishes and explaining why a posthumous edition of his greatest work is not dedicated in print, as it must be in the hearts of all his friends, to THOMAS ASHBY'.[32]

In the decade since the war had ended, Ashby's life, which had possessed a steady direction to it up until that time, had seemingly become confused, with financial survival proving a constant preoccupation. The completion of *Aqueducts* through the winter of 1930–1 clearly had been an ordeal, achieved despite his deteriorating eyesight as well as poor health (Fig. 34).[33] Ian Richmond recorded that in April 1931, three weeks before he died, 'he had deposited with the Clarendon Press the manuscript of a topographical study in 925 foolscap pages ... it is well known that he considered it to be his life-work'.[34] Hence, when he reached England in May 1931, he may well have dwelt upon where the coming years would lead him.

Ralegh Radford believed that he met Ashby at Richborough in 1931, a week before he died. Although this seems improbable, there can be little doubt that the encounter dated to Ashby's last years. Bushe-Fox, the excavator of Richborough, had no desire to speak with Ashby, whom he did not take to, so delegated Radford to act as his guide. Radford recalled that he was in fine form, with no intimation of any psychological problems.[35]

On 18 May 1931 news of Ashby's death was conveyed by Evelyn Shaw to Rennell Rodd. The letter was a harbinger of a flurry of correspondence over the coming months:

> You will be sorry to read in *The Times* today of Ashby's death. I believe he fell out of a train on his way to Oxford, but I do not know this for certain.
>
> I think that our friend Mrs Strong may possibly make this an excuse to tell the public through *The Times* that his retirement from the School under circumstances so undignified to the authorities that they cannot at this juncture be properly mentioned was the cause of the illness that eventually brought about his death.

Eugénie Strong remained silent. Shaw, however, took no chances. Once more he was stage-managing matters. It is doubtful that the School Secretary was surprised by a letter from Arthur Smith, dated 18 July 1931, in which the former Chairman of the Faculty of Archaeology, History and Letters explained how Sir Frederick Kenyon (director of the British Museum) had asked him to undertake a

memoir of Ashby for the *Proceedings of the British Academy*: 'I am sending you a draft of what I propose to say about the non-reappointment episode'.

Smith's draft was swiftly reworked by Shaw. The original memoir read:

> The question of renewal in 1925 came up for examination in 1924, and the Executive decided not to renew. It is perhaps permissible now to say that the main factors were dissatisfaction on the part of the representatives of the Art Faculties, and a general feeling that the machinery of direction worked with undue friction. It must be allowed that Ashby had not, either by instinct or training, the gift of ordered routine conducive to the smooth running of an institution. The representatives of Archaeology, History and Letters acquiesced in the decision, but did not either initiate or advocate it.
>
> The notification came as a surprise, and disappointment but was accepted by Ashby with dignified silence. From what has been said above it will be seen that no question of dismissal or resignation arose. In view, however, of the fact that the cosmopolitan Roman public could not be expected to grasp niceties of procedure, Ashby and his friends were sorry that he was not invited to withdraw his candidature, and so to effect an approximation to the latter alternative.

A flurry of correspondence was generated by Smith's memoir. From the 'London' archives of the School come the following letters:

> Mr Shaw:
> *Re Smith's Note on Dr. Ashby*
>   I thought I sent you attached to Smith's Note a copy of all the Ex: Cttee Minutes dealing with Ashby's appointment and retirement. However here is the whole file. Richmond said he would write to you about his disagreement with Smith's line. Richmond wanted to be too honest in that the real reason for dismissal was the quarrelling of two women! but agreed that this would raise a hornet's nest and probably loose [sic] us the Ashby library!!
> Stanley[36]
> 31–7–31.

> 5th. August 1931
> My Dear Smith,
>   I hope you will not mind my amending your draft about Ashby. I think it unwise to attempt to tell the truth which we did our best officially to disguise. Your words strike me as being rather harsh and might appear to others as being even aggressive and as the whole trouble has now been forgotten, it would, in my view, be a mistake and fundamentally wrong to blame Ashby's capacity or personal qualities as a Director when his damnably silly wife's bickering with Mrs Strong was the sole cause of his retirement.
>   Besides, Richmond is trying, and I believe successfully, to make Mrs Ashby his friend, and if we said anything that would bring her and

Mrs Strong together again, our prospects of getting Ashby's library would vanish.[37]

Your words, moreover, clearly suggest that the writer must have been behind the scenes, and I do not feel that, as the Executive Committee have gone out of their way to say nothing about the real cause, nothing should be said about it until some angel finds a formula to satisfy the scruples of all concerned.

Yours ever,

Evelyn Shaw

Milnrow, Rochdale 6. viii '31.

My dear Shaw,

I have been at work all morning on this very tentative draft of a very thorny question; and I think that I have arrived at a version which comes very near the truth, without stating it, and which one side would read as though we were rather sorry, while the other would judge that we were sticking to our guns; and silence, anyhow, is enjoined by Ashby's example!! I also think that any outsider must see from it that personal questions lie behind it all. But I want you to go over it very carefully, weighing each word; and then you will probably substitute something better of your own ...

With best wishes to you all,

Ian A. Richmond

P.S. If you use this draft, do not send it to Smith as my suggestion. I had rather not appear in the matter. Say you have been thinking it over & this appeals to you, or something of that sort.

The amended draft was agreed as follows:[38]

The first appointment to the Directorship of the incorporated School dated from 1910, for a term of three years. It was no part of the scheme of the Executive Committee that there should be an automatic renewal. It was made, however, without question in 1913, and through the war period in 1915, 1919 and 1922. The question of renewal in 1925 came up for examination in 1924 and it was then that the Executive Committee decided only to renew Ashby's appointment for a further year after the expiration of his current term of office.

Much has been said in criticism of this action of the authorities which was dictated in the interests of the School as a whole, and if the notification came as a surprise and disappointment to Ashby, he nevertheless accepted it in that spirit of unquestioning loyalty which was always one of the finest traits in his character.

Shaw's generally skilful handling of the issue did not mask the sadness of the situation. The School's annual budget climbed steadily from £2,677 in 1919–20 to over £8,642 in Ashby's last year as Director. By 1931 it had failed to grow any more, and the published accounts reveal an operating budget of £8,183. The figures reflect the problems suffered by Ashby's successors. Bernard Ashmole

had been unable to take to Rome, and left after making no real mark in 1928 to take up the Yates Chair of Archaeology at University College, London.[39] Arthur Smith, aged 68, had been despatched as an interim Director. Despite his lifelong, intimate association with the School, his spell in the office was undistinguished. Alan Sorrell, a painter-scholar at this time, lampooned him as follows in a scene set at Christmas dinner in 1928:[40] 'They're going, and Gunter calls for 'Three cheers for Dr. and Mrs. Hamley', and three sadly ironical salutations are given, and the Doctor acknowledges them with a half turn and a mayoral wave of the hand which makes the order suspended round his neck glint in a manner somehow reminiscent of the Agricultural Show'.

Ian Richmond, Ashby's pupil, was a more appropriate appointment to the Directorship. He assumed responsibility for the School in 1930, at the age of 28. That year, his *The City Wall of Imperial Rome: an Account of its Architectural Development from Aurelian to Narses* appeared — a study that, he acknowledged, owed much to Ashby's support.[41] Richmond succeeded with May Ashby. Ashby's books and photographs were made over to the British School on 3 October 1931, May Ashby stipulating that 'the collection as it stands must never be divided nor allowed to leave Rome'.[42] Richmond also persuaded May Ashby to loan the School all Ashby's remarkable collection of manuscripts and prints. Access to this was to be at Richmond's discretion. May Ashby generously continued to pay the insurance on the collection. This arrangement, however, was to be short-lived. Richmond was compelled to quit the School at short notice the following autumn, and once again Arthur Smith was back in charge. As a result, May Ashby lost patience with the School, and, recalling her late husband's lifelong esteem for the Vatican Library and for Franz Ehrle, its Prefect from 1895 to 1913, she offered the collection to Monsignor (later Cardinal) Tisserant in February 1933. By mid-March an accord had been reached, and Tisserant duly sent a cheque for 48,000 lire. An additional sum of 14,000 lire was subsequently paid after May Ashby insisted that the Vatican take possession of all the collection.

The then Director of the School, Colin Hardie, felt he had been duped by the clever Monsignor Tisserant. Recalling the incident in 1992, he believed himself to be guilty of incompetence. The reality was a little different. Hardie had made a positive effort to cauterize the wounds left after Richmond's departure. But May Ashby was a difficult person with whom to deal, as she had had enough of the British School. Tisserant played the situation to the Vatican's advantage.[43] Four hundred and forty-seven priceless items passed to the Vatican, their worth only becoming apparent with the publication of Raymond Keaveney's *Views of Rome* in 1988. May Ashby used the money to move to the Royal Pavilion Hotel, Folkestone, and then to London, where she lived throughout the '30s, becoming a rotund woman with a high-pitched voice, according to her niece. Meanwhile, so Ralegh Radford recalled, Evelyn Shaw was made to wait for his recognition for his work for the School. His knighthood

came in 1947, on his retirement as Secretary of the School, rather late in life because, Radford surmised, he was held culpable for the Executive Committee's decision in 1924. Writing to his successor, Admiral Anthony James, on 14 January 1972, Sir Evelyn, aged 90, gave his version of these searing events in the School's history:

> I disliked Mrs Ashby as much as I liked her husband who was utterly loyal but too innocent to suspect the dishonest motives of his wife. As the Director's wife Mrs Ashby expected to take possession of Mrs Arthur Strong & this in the end led to an open dispute which disturbed the peace of the whole school. After getting reports on the rumpus from Rome scholars I told Lord Esher that I could no longer control the worsening situation & that the only thing to be done was to rid ourselves of Ashby his wife & Mrs Strong & replace them with a younger man (Ashmole). He readily agreed & promised to take full responsibility for the plan if I would engineer it. So we appointed a small subcommittee of Mrs Strong's firm friends (Kenyon, Crawford, Rodd etc.) & laid before them all the correspondence that had passed between me and the School during the previous few months. The committee were so appalled at what I had endured that they unanimously endorsed Esher's proposal 'to sack the lot'. In this way we entered into a period of undisturbed peace.

6

Ashby's Legacy

Mi sembra di sentire la voce di un mio antico
produttore: 'Ma come, finisce cosi ... senza un
filo di speranza, un raggio di sole? Ma dammi
almeno un raggio di sole', mi supplicava alle
prime proiezioni dei miei film ... Un raggio di
sole? Mah, non so, proviamo.

Scene 46 of *Intervista* from Federico Fellini,
Block-Notes di Un Regista (Milan, 1988), 182[1]

Ashby's work has stood the test of time; indeed, admiration for his scholarship
has never been greater. In the '30s and '40s Giuseppe Lugli, perhaps the most
distinguished Italian topographer of this period, kept Ashby's name alive. As late
as 1946 he wrote an affectionate essay recalling their days out walking in the
Campagna Romana.[2] Thus a baton from the past was conspicuously passed on
to the new generation of archaeologists of the post-1945 era. Italian topographers
were highly appreciative of Ashby's achievement. Lorenzo Quilici, for example,
cogently has summed up Ashby's legacy as follows: '[his] topographic research
remains unsurpassed and often today constitutes the last authoritative word on
academic arguments which had previously been much debated'.[3] Yet it is the
British tradition of topographic studies in Italy that has had the greatest
international resonance. Foremost in this field was the first Director of the British
School after the end of the Second World War — John Ward-Perkins.

Ward-Perkins, a Craven Scholar in the '30s, was made Director of the British
School in 1945. Though too young to have known Ashby, he inherited Bruno
Bonelli, the School's steward, who had been appointed in Ashby's last years at the
School. Ward-Perkins no doubt had met Eugénie Strong in the '30s, though she
died in Rome during the war. To begin with, Ward-Perkins concerned himself
mostly with the Roman archaeology of North Africa. But in 1955 he launched a
field survey of South Etruria that retraced some of Ashby's intellectual steps. In the
first of many reports on this project, Ward-Perkins wrote:[4]

The romantic desolation of Southern Etruria is being transformed from
one day to the next under the impact of a scheme of land-reform
comparable in scale to the great reforms of classical antiquity, and vast

estates which for centuries have been used for stock-breeding and
seasonal pasture are being broken up and brought into cultivation with
all the devastating thoroughness that modern mechanical equipment
entails ... Much of the damage to ancient sites is unavoidable, the
inevitable accompaniment of any scheme to put the land to agricultural
use ... The moral is ... if this material is to be recorded, the record
must be made at once.

The destruction anticipated by Ashby was happening. For twenty years Ward-
Perkins's teams carried out surveys of the region, setting a standard that was to be
the basis for countless other archaeological surveys throughout central Italy. The
new topographers examined every field for the archaeology of all periods — from
the Palaeolithic to the modern age. Ward-Perkins was instrumental in developing
a long-term history for the hinterland of Rome, something which contrasts with
Ashby's work, which had concentrated upon one episode only — the late
Republican–early Imperial period.

Ward-Perkins's successors have sustained the high standing of British
archaeology in Italy and also appreciated the work of their predecessors. In 1986
Graeme Barker, the then Director of the British School, identified Ashby as the
founding father of the tradition of archaeological survey later developed by
Ward-Perkins and, indeed, himself.[5] David Whitehouse, Director between 1974
and 1983, elaborated Barker's analysis in a *postilla*, illustrating Ashby's place in
the history of field survey in Italy.[6] Ashby's achievement was most
conspicuously evaluated in a major photographic exhibition masterminded by
Francesco Castagnoli, a student of Lugli's and a renowed topographer. The
exhibition, entitled *Thomas Ashby: un archeologo fotografa la Campagna
Romana fra '800 e '900*, was mounted at the British School at Rome in 1986 and
sponsored by the Istituto Centrale per il Catalogo e la Documentazione, which
now holds Ashby's 9,000 negatives.[7] Afterwards, the exhibition toured several
British universities. A second exhibition concerned with Ashby's photographs of
Rome, entitled *Archeologia a Roma nelle fotografie di Thomas Ashby 1891–
1930*, followed the same route in 1989;[8] a third took place in 1994, on *Il Lazio
di Thomas Ashby 1891–1930*.[9]

Meanwhile, Ashby's legacy in other fields has come under similar scrutiny.
The Vatican Library, in collaboration with the Smithsonian, held an exhibition of
Ashby's watercolour and print collection (given to the Vatican in 1933) in 1988,
entitled *Views of Rome*.[10] This exhibition then travelled around several centres
in the United States of America. Since then, Ashby's posthumous study of
aqueducts has been translated into Italian (1991),[11] and the on-going project on
the late Renaissance collector Cassiano dal Pozzo involves publishing much of
Ashby's research.[12] In Wales, new excavations at Caerwent have inevitably
meant a reappraisal of Ashby's campaigns. Emptying his old trenches, like
publishing the Executive Committee's reports on his Directorship of the School,
is discomforting and intrusive. Yet, as George Boon has shown, Ashby's

FIG. 35. The demolition of the Villa di Domiziano (Casale di Vicarello, Bracciano), 1912.
(British School at Rome Archive Neg. No. XLI,92 (GFN H 3515))

reputation has survived the test, revealing him to have been an able field archaeologist.[13]

    In short, more than half a century after his death, there is high regard for Ashby's work. Why is this? There are several interrelated reasons. Firstly, as we have seen, the profound quality of Ashby's work is indisputable. Secondly, the value of Ashby's archive has been appreciated. It is a modest treasure-house: the product of prodigious energy, combined with a gift of recording in his notebooks, by photography and, of course, in published form (Figs 35–8). He was a late Grand Tourist, witnessing the transformation of early modern Rome into a modern capital and the taming of the Roman Campagna. His record of this age is priceless. Thirdly, the British School at Rome (and the academics associated with it) feels quite remote from its founders and from the conflicts of the '20s. Ashby is, therefore, the subject of abstract, almost objective, fascination. Indeed, rather like the Merchant–Ivory films of E.M. Forster's novels, Ashby's age conveys a sense of morality, stability and, erroneously, a Britain in ascendency remote from the troubled nation of today, with its perceived devaluation of academic traditions. Moreover, the British School at Rome has needed to identify its roots as well as direction. Its original purposes, described in Chapter Three, no longer exactly hold true in the age of Apex travel, European Community programmes, and, especially, a post-modern ethos. Ashby's research provides a rich (and fertile) foundation for the School's existence. Above all, it is also a marketable commodity. Italian *enti* are disposed to fund the research, publication and exhibition of Ashby's work because his photographs record a lost Italy. In a time when British institutions must justify their existence as much by income generation as by their activities, this source of revenue has proved an invaluable asset for the otherwise potentially rootless British School.

All these activities have placed Ashby under an academic spotlight, however, that this modest man would not have anticipated and probably would not have appreciated. Lanciani, of course, is still revered in Italy, though scarcely known to students of archaeology elsewhere. Pelham, Myres, Smith and the founding fathers of the British School have been virtually forgotten. Indeed, in most cases only the building in the Valle Giulia causes their names from time to time to be recalled, invariably in Ashby's slipstream.

FIG. 36. Tufa quarries at Tor Cervara, abandoned since antiquity, with two carts (*barozze*) drawn by bulls, 22 January 1896. *(British School at Rome Archive Neg. No. 565)*

FIG. 37. The Tiber in the stretch between Ponte Palatino and Testaccio, probably taken from the garden of the church of Sant'Alessio, 1915. *(British School at Rome Archive Neg. No. XLVIII,19 (GFN H 4134))*

Ashby was much more than a late Grand Tourist. The new research has revealed him to be a perceptive bridge between antiquarians and modern archaeologists. Ashby was fortunate in his training — his *formazione*. His father introduced him to the exquisite rural beauty of central Italy at an early age and fostered his interest in antiquity. While still a teenager, Ashby senior undoubtedly introduced his son to the British and American Archaeological Society in the early 1890s, and, most importantly, to Rodolfo Lanciani. A decade later, in 1903, Ashby senior also ensured that the British School was sufficiently funded to afford his son as Assistant Director. With this modest private independence, Ashby was freed from the treadmill of tutoring, the fate that befell many later Victorian Oxbridge graduates in Greats. The importance of Ashby's benign, Quaker, father in his life cannot be overstated. His more devout mother, by contrast, although she and her son lived together for almost a decade before the First World War and for a brief period afterwards, remains an enigma.

Fundamental to his formation was his Oxford training. He was a pupil of Haverfield, who had been the principle student of Henry Pelham. Haverfield was inspired by Theodor Mommsen, who was developing the German classical

FIG. 38. The Tiber in flood near San Michele, with the Janiculum in the background, 1915.
(British School at Rome Archive Neg. No. XLVIII,18 (GFN H 4135))

tradition in its own, imaginative creed. Haverfield, in particular, taught Ashby the discipline of archaeological enquiry — something that was virtually unknown at this time. The methodological emphasis upon historical training, material culture and, above all, interdisciplinary collaboration was to be the hallmark of Ashby's career.

Ashby's research was always following a thread that he himself had spun, but it was embroidered by the constancy of his companions (Fig. 39). Lanciani, more than anyone else, provided him with a boundless intellectual enquiry that spanned almost his entire career. Nevertheless, without offence being taken, he was able to associate with Lanciani's great competitor, Giacomo Boni, as Boni's biographer recalled with admiration.[14] Other companions provided invaluable friendship: Franz Ehrle, the prefect of the Vatican, Alfred Hudd at Caerwent, Eric Peet and Themistocles Zammit on Malta, F.G. Newton, the architect who drew many of his discoveries, Duncan Mackenzie on Sardinia, Esther Van Deman on aqueducts, and, latterly, R.A. Fell, Giuseppe Lugli and Ian Richmond, as Ashby worked once more on the Roman Campagna. And there were many more besides, as Tomassetti's bibliographic study of Ashby's career illustrates.[15] Yet it

FIG. 39. Thomas Ashby (second from right) beside a Roman
mausoleum near Nettuno. *(British School at Rome
Archive Neg. No. TA 775)*

would be mistaken to cast these colleagues as collaborators; they were sounding-boards providing Ashby with techniques and intellectual debate as he pursued his chosen path. Yet Ashby's company was evidently cherished, as was shown in Chapter One. His companionship, if sometimes seemingly unworldly, was memorable because it held the key to a world that conspicuously was being eclipsed.

But inevitably his professional formation was overshadowed by worldly circumstances. Ashby, we need to remind ourselves, was the last member of a family of brewers. Nevertheless, his father played a significant part in his career in so far as Thomas Ashby senior quit his mercantile background for early retirement in Italy, releasing his son at an early age from the prospect of a career in business. Ashby senior was unusual. Norma Clarke has provided a cogent description of the normal conflicts of this age:[16]

> The thrusting mercantile middle classes of the nineteenth century tended to view the product intellectuals produced as of minimal value. In the popular perspective, intellectual life equalled 'unprofitably utilised leisure', the amateurish pursuit of knowledge for its own sake instead of economically profitable appropriation of knowledge. As such, ... it was acceptable activity for middle-class women whose leisure was a significant sign of their husband's prosperity; but a young man unprofitably engaged was in danger of being drawn into feminine social roles. G.M. Young, looking back on the Victorian period from the 1950s, certainly thought that there had been a feminizing of intellectual work and a consequent (and regrettable) loss of virility. Their fathers, he observed of the mid-Victorian public, had been better men.

How true was this of Ashby? His life, despite his father's best intentions, was dogged by his institutional pedigree. He was caught between an expatriate world of post-Garibaldian romanticism and decadent late Victorian education and management. His energetic approach to life seems to have stemmed from his time at Winchester, where idleness was equated with a propensity to sexual perversion. Idleness only began to cause him anxiety at the end of the '20s, when he suffered from illness. From his first photographic album, dating from 1891–2, an eclectic curiosity in antiquity, places, peoples and their ethnography, and in his family is exposed (Fig. 40). He also liked to appear in photographs, offering a bold pose for the camera. These photographs expose someone who liked to strike a contrived, if slightly unusual, appearance. Hence he was remembered for his idiosyncratic walking attire (above, Figs 2, 8 and 31). There was, then, a streak of schooled arrogance that diminished with age and distance from British institutional life.

Ashby drew his strength from his enduring relationship with Italy. Although he wrote nothing about this, his assessment of Turner, taken from Ruskin's essay, possibly serves to illustrate his attitude:[17]

> The effect of Italy upon his [Turner's] mind is very puzzling (wrote Ruskin). On the one hand it gave him the solemnity and power which are manifested in the historical compositions of the Liber Studiorum — on the other, he never seems to have entered thoroughly into the spirit of Italy, and the materials he obtained there were afterwards but awkwardly introduced into his larger compositions ... The chief reason of these failures I imagine to be the effort of the artist to put joyousness and brilliancy of effect upon scenes eminently pensive, to substitute radiance for serenity of light, and to force the freedom and

breadth of line which he learnt to love on English downs and Highland
moors, out of a country dotted by campaniles and square convents,
bristled with cypresses, partitioned by walls, and gone up and down by
steps.

Ashby understood Italy in the tradition of British liberals like George Trevelyan,
but, unlike Trevelyan, he could extend that empathy to Italians. He was more than
a Grand Tourist in this sense. But inevitably this empathy coloured his relations
with British scholars, who, Bernard Ashmole reminds us, were 'apt to give
themselves airs' in the British School.[18]

Ashby's weaknesses are equally plain to see. The gruff Ashby who was
fortunate to be elected Director of the School, the young awkward site director at
Caerwent, the unsettling early years as Director before the arrival of Eugénie
Strong in 1909, and the somewhat aloof character recalled in the '20s — these
are all tell-tale reflections of a sad conflict in Ashby's life. The apparent absence
of his mother in the world projected by him, the telling, matronly, role of Eugénie
Strong in her stead and then her significant eclipse by May Price-Williams to
some extent reveals a much missed need for female companionship and, with it, a
home. Eugénie Strong undoubtedly understood his plight, not least because she
held him in great intellectual esteem. The striking romanticism of her dedication
of *Apotheosis and the After-life* to Christian Mallet illustrates the power of her
emotions. She was a Catholic, he of Quaker parentage. They were binary
opposites in so many matters. Nevertheless, perhaps because of her instinctive
attachment to Ashby, she could not help but scorn May Ashby's desire to run the
School and to make it into a comfortable home. Added to this, Eugénie Strong
viewed the poseur with a rather ironic eye and was not so much pained as puzzled
by Philistines.[19]

The triangular relations with Eugénie Strong and his wife were cruelly
exposed in the confined circumstances of the British School. Here he was
unknowingly confronting a choice between a normal relationship and a quasi-
monastic life as a scholar caring for an institute. The choice came at a perilous
time. The 'Old England of the cathedrals and ancient universities, and the
industrial community of coal, iron and steel, was being Americanised by cinema,
bungalows, arterial and by-pass roads and Woolworths'.[20] All this was quite
alien to this introspective archaeologist, but seductive to his wife. By this time,
too, with his father long-since dead and with the untimely death of Francis
Haverfield, Ashby, in conflict with Eugénie Strong, was bereft of a mentor on
such matters. Arthur Smith's analysis of Ashby's apartment in 1924 and of his
wife's wish for more rooms is touched with comic pathos. The grandees of the
Executive Committee had lost any familiarity with the creature they had created.
In the confusion of late Victorian ethics, scholarship had become equated with
poverty. May Ashby became a scapegoat for the ineffectiveness of the Executive
Committee at raising funds for the new institute. Their anachronistic ethics are

FIG. 40. Donkey market at Aquila. *(British School at Rome Archive Neg. No. TA 1405)*

enshrined in the plan and arrangement of the British School at Rome. Cheaply made late imperial grandeur concealed a meanly constructed hostel, or, as the playwright Alan Bennett put it, 'much of Lutyens's architecture is as contemptuous of the individual as the bleakest tower block'.[21] The design of the British School was inward-looking, away from the troubled daily life of Italy. Ashby's fate was to be an expatriate who had a genuine love of Italy, but who spent much of his life leading an institution that paradoxically challenged his own spirit.

Thomas Ashby will never have a commanding place in the hall of archaeological fame. He does not rank alongside the British masters in this field, Arthur Evans, Vere Gordon Childe, Francis Haverfield, Mortimer Wheeler and Leonard Wooley, even if he deserves to do so. Nevertheless, his contribution with Rodolfo Lanciani to the discovery of ancient Rome ranks with the highest historical scholarship. After all, theirs was the fortune to chart a great episode of world history. Following in the footsteps of the great Grand Tourists — painters, collectors such as Cassiano dal Pozzo, Lord Bristol and Thomas Jenkins, as well as antiquarians like Gell and Dennis — Ashby deployed the media known to him, the written word, studies of drawings and prints, and photographs, to record a past that was conspicuously menaced by modernity. If Ashby had lived out a natural life, I believe that in his later years his achievement would have been truly recognized in Britain. The *raggio di sole* is that, unlike many in the hall of archaeological fame, Ashby's legacy has an enduring quality that, as we have seen, has given it a contemporary currency in Italy. In this sense, to paraphrase his friend, Giuseppe Lugli, the adventures of the expatriate pupil of Haverfield exceeded normal, modest, purport, but a sadness forever attaches to his ending.[22]

NOTES

Primary sources

The British School at Rome currently has two uncatalogued archives: firstly, the papers, photographs and other belongings of Thomas Ashby and other residents of the School, and, secondly, an administrative archive compiled in London by the Schcol's Secretaries. Both archives are in Rome. Unless otherwise stated, all the letters referred to here, such as those sent to Evelyn Shaw by Thomas Ashby and Eugénie Strong, are in the files of the 'London office', filed by the year.

Abbreviations

Ashby, *Aqueducts*	Thomas Ashby, *The Aqueducts of Ancient Rome* (Oxford, 1935)
Ashby, *Campagna*	Thomas Ashby, *The Roman Campagna in Classical Times* (London, 1970 (new edition) with an introduction by John Ward-Perkins)
PBSR	*Papers of the British School at Rome*
Smith (1931)	A.H. Smith, 'Thomas Ashby, 1874–1931', *Proceedings of the British Academy* 17 (1931), 515–41
Tomassetti (1927)	F. Tomassetti, 'Scrittori contemporanei di cose romane: Thomas Ashby', *Archivio della Reale Società Romana di Storia Patria* (1927), 77–123
Wiseman (1990)	T.P. Wiseman, *A Short History of the British School at Rome* (London, 1990)

TO PREFACE

1. D.H. Lawrence in a letter to A.W. McLeod, in Aldous Huxley (ed.), *The Letters of D.H. Lawrence* (London, 1932), 119–20.
2. Wiseman (1990), published in a slightly different form in P. Vian (ed.), *Speculum Mundi. Roma centro internazionale di ricerche umanistiche* (Rome, 1992), 81–121.

TO CHAPTER ONE

1. Quoted by May Ashby in her foreword to Thomas Ashby, *The Aqueducts of Ancient Rome* (Oxford, 1935), v.
2. Smith (1931: 528) recorded that he was on his way to Oxford; see also E.A. Winslow, *A Libation to the Gods: the Story of the Roman Aqueducts* (London, 1963), xv. Ashby must have intended to change trains in London, proceeding from Paddington to Oxford.
3. *The Times* 21 May 1931.
4. Ralegh Radford in an interview with the author on 19 July 1991 believed that Ashby did *not* commit suicide. He suspected that Ashby had simply opened the wrong door. Radford believed that he had seen Ashby the previous week, when he had visited Radford on J.P. Bushe-Fox's excavations of the Roman supply fort at Richborough (Kent). He recalled him as being perfectly normal. Radford repeated this view in a letter to the author of 21 January 1994. It seems likely that Radford was in fact recalling an earlier visit to Richborough, while Ashby and his wife were holidaying at St Margaret's Bay, Dover.
5. Tomassetti, 1927: 77–8.

6. The photographic albums are housed in the archives of the British School at Rome; the negatives are held by the Istituto Centrale per il Catalogo e la Documentazione, Rome.
7. See John Pemble, *The Mediterranean Passion. Victorians and Edwardians in the South* (Oxford, 1987), 268.
8. Smith, 1931: 521.
9. See G.H. Hallam, 'Notes on the cult of Hercules Victor in Tibur and its neighbourhood', *Journal of Roman Studies* 21 (1931), 276–82, at p. 276.
10. Winslow, *A Libation to the Gods* (above, n. 2), xii–xv.
11. Smith, 1931: 529.
12. John Ward-Perkins, 'Foreword' to Ashby, *Campagna*, viii.
13. Donna Kurtz (ed.), *Bernard Ashmole, 1894–1988. An Autobiography* (Oxford, 1994), 42.
14. Cited by Smith (1931: 529–30).
15. Giuseppe Lugli, 'Piccole avventure romane di un archeologo militante', *Strenna di Romanisti* 7 (1946), 42–50; Ward-Perkins, 'Foreword' (above, n. 12), vii, recorded that Ashby 'shaped the tastes and talents of the young Giuseppe Lugli'.
16. *The Letters of Gertrude Bell* (Harmondsworth, 1927), vol. ii, 256.
17. Wiseman, 1990: 16.
18. The letters of Winifred Knights are held in the archive of the Strang Print Room of the Slade, University College, London. I am grateful to Nicola Kadinsky, the curator, for her help in copying the letters.
19. See Karin Einaudi (ed.), *Esther B. Van Deman: Images from the Archive of an American Archaeologist at the Turn of the Century* (Rome, 1991), 23, fig. 45.
20. See a letter from Eugénie Strong to Evelyn Shaw, dated 13 December 1916, in the archives of the British School at Rome.
21. *Tenth Annual Report of the Managing Committee (of the British School at Rome) 1909–10*, 2.
22. See Susanna Le Pera Buranelli and Rita Turchetti, 'Gli appunti di Thomas Ashby', in *Archeologia a Roma nelle fotografie di Thomas Ashby 1891–1930* (Naples, 1989), 156–7. Some of the notes are transcribed on pp. 158–88 of that volume.
23. Ian Richmond, 'Editor's note', in Ashby, *Aqueducts*, vi, n. 1.
24. Ashby's own copies of *PBSR* traditionally have been held in the Director's office in the School.
25. G.M. Trevelyan, 'Walking', in G.M. Trevelyan, *Clio a Muse and Other Essays* (London, 1930), 1–18, at p. 6.
26. Cited by David Cannadine, *G.M. Trevelyan. A Life in History* (London, 1932), 149.
27. D.H. Lawrence to A.W. McLeod on 26 April 1913, in Aldous Huxley (ed.), *The Letters of D.H. Lawrence* (London, 1932), 119–20.
28. Figures taken from E.J. Hobsbawn, *The Age of Empire 1875–1914* (Harmondsworth, 1989), table 2.
29. C.F.C. Masterman, *The Condition of England* (London, 1909), 203.
30. G.M. Trevelyan, 'The white peril', *Nineteenth Century* 1 (1901), 1,043–55.
31. Ashby, *Campagna*, respectively pp. 53 and 52. Lorenzo Quilici lamented the fact that Ashby concentrated upon the archaeology of the regions well outside the suburban overspill (*periferia*) (presumably where it was most pleasant to walk): 'La villa nel suburbio romano: problemi di studio e di inquadramento storico-topografico', *Archeologica Classica* 31 (1979), 309–17, at p. 313.
32. Leonard Woolley, *Dead Towns and Living Men. Being Pages from an Antiquary's Notebook* (Oxford, 1925), 48–9.
33. Unpublished letters of Winifred Knights in the Strang Print Room (see n. 18).
34. Thomas Ashby, 'The Latin Shore', *The Independent* October 28 1909, 969–76 at p. 974.
35. Thomas Ashby, 'Scrittori contemporanei di cose romane: Rodolfo Lanciani', *Archivio della Reale Società Romana di Storia Patria* 51 (1928), 103–43, at p. 126.
36. Tea Martinelli, 'Le collezione fotografica', in *Thomas Ashby. Un archeologo fotografa la Campagna Romana tra '800 e '900* (British School at Rome Archive 1) (Rome, 1986), 12.
37. Cf. Pierre Bourdieu, *Photography. A Middle-brow Art* (Cambridge, 1990), 41.
38. On Esther Van Deman see Einaudi, *Esther B. Van Deman* (above, n. 19).
39. See Maria Cecilia Mazzi, 'Sulle orme di Thomas Ashby: piccole storie di grandi collezioni', in *Il Lazio di Thomas Ashby 1891–1930* (British School at Rome Archive 4) (Rome, 1994), 17–31, at

pp. 17 and 30–1.

40. Tea Martinelli, 'Macchine fotografiche e negativi', in *Thomas Ashby. Un archeologo fotografa la Campagna Romana tra '800 e '900 (British School at Rome Archive* 1) (Rome, 1986), 13.

41. Martinelli, 'Macchine fotografiche e negativi' (above, n. 40), 13.

42. Thomas Ashby, 'Applicazione della fotografia aerea agli studi archeologici', *Reale Accademia Nazionale dei Lincei* 32 (1923), 186–7.

TO CHAPTER TWO

1. Smith, 1931: 515, quoting from Robert Ashby, *Pedigree of the Ashbys of Staines, 1523–1918,* in the Library of the Society of Friends.

2. See A.O. Prickard, 'Life in "Commoners"', in 'Old Wykehamists', *Winchester College 1393–1893* (London, 1893), 112–15.

3. My thanks to Dr Peter Partner for this information.

4. See Norman Sherry, *The Life of Graham Greene,* Vol. 1, *1904–1933* (Harmondsworth, 1990), 41.

5. See G.H. Hallam, 'Notes on the cult of Hercules Victor in Tibur and its neighbourhood', *Journal of Roman Studies* 21 (1931), 276–82, at p. 276; Ashby dedicated 'The classical topography of the Roman Campagna — II', *PBSR* 3 (1906), 1–212, at pp. 6–7, to Searle. In her obituary of Thomas Ashby, Eugénie Strong recorded that he had been in Italy since the age of 14: *Annales Institutorum* 3 (1930–1), 7–8, at p. 7.

6. John Pemble, *The Mediterranean Passion. Victorians and Edwardians in the South* (Oxford, 1987), 275.

7. See Duncan Wilson, *Gilbert Murray* (Oxford, 1987), 19–20.

8. Quoted in Smith, 1931: 517.

9. Quoted in Smith, 1931: 517.

10. George MacDonald, 'Francis Haverfield', *Proceedings of the British Academy* 9 (1919–20), 475–91; see also H.H.E. Craster, 'Francis Haverfield', *English Historical Review* 35 (1920), 63–70, who described Mommsen as his master on pp. 63–4. See Francis Haverfield, 'Theodor Mommsen', *English Historical Review* 19 (1904), 80–9: 'Mommsen did more than any scholar living or dead to extend the range of historical inquiry to archaeological regions' (p. 86). I am grateful to Philip Freeman for his advice on Francis Haverfield and for making his research available to me.

11. T.P. Wiseman, 'Con Boni nel foro: i diari romani di W. St. Clair Baddeley', *Rivista dell'Istituto Nazionale di Archeologia e Storia dell'Arte* 8–9 (1985–6), 119–49, at p. 126.

12. George C. Boon, 'Archaeology through the Severn Tunnel: the Caerwent Exploration Fund, 1899–1917', *Transactions of the Bristol and Gloucestershire Archaeological Society* 107 (1989), 5–26, at p. 9.

13. Quoted from Francis Haverfield's Ford lectures published in F. Haverfield and G. MacDonald, *The Roman Occupation of Britain* (Oxford, 1924), 85–7; and F. Haverfield, 'Inaugural address to the Roman Society', *Journal of Roman Studies* 1 (1911), xi–xx, at pp. xviii–xix.

14. P. Levine, *The Amateur and the Professional* (Cambridge, 1986), 34–5.

15. Quoted from J. Mulvaney, 'Another university man gone wrong', in D.R. Harris (ed.), *The Archaeology of V. Gordon Childe. Contemporary Perspectives* (London, 1994), 55–74, at pp. 67–8.

16. See T.J. Dunbabin, 'Sir John Myres, 1869–1954', *Proceedings of the British Academy* 41 (1955), 349–65, at p. 350.

17. See B. Trigger, *A History of Archaeological Thought* (Cambridge, 1989), 148–206.

18. Dunbabin, 'Sir John Myres' (above, n. 16).

19. Tomassetti, 1927: 78, n. 1; on postgraduate degrees in archaeology at Oxford University see Levine, *The Amateur and the Professional* (above, n. 14), 157.

20. Mark Bowden, *The Life and Archaeological Work of Lieutenant–General Augustus Henry Lane Fox Pitt Rivers DCL, FRS, FSA* (Cambridge, 1991); Haverfield and MacDonald, *The*

Roman Occupation of Britain (above, n. 13), 87.

21. George C. Boon, *Silchester, the Roman Town of Calleva* (London, 1974).

22. Boon, *Silchester* (above, n. 21), 30.

23. Boon, 'Caerwent Exploration Fund' (above, n. 12), 9.

24. I am greatly indebted to George Boon, who discovered this unpublished doggerel amongst the Caerwent Exploration Fund papers in Newport Museum.

25. Unpublished letter in Newport Museum. I owe its discovery to George Boon, who kindly made the transcription for me.

26. I am very grateful to Richard Brewer of the National Museum of Wales for his guidance on Ashby's excavations at Caerwent; Mr Brewer's excavations are described in *Britannia* 18 (1987), 308–9; 19 (1988), 422–3; 20 (1989), 264; 21 (1990), 307–10; 22 (1991), 225–6; 22 (1992), 258–9; 24 (1993), 275; 25 (1994), 251–2; Sir Leonard Woolley, recalling his experiences at Corbridge, cast doubts on Haverfield's management of excavations in *Spadework* (London, 1953), 14.

27. Boon, 'Caerwent Exploration Fund' (above, n. 12), 14.

28. Quoted in D. Manacorda and R. Tamassia, *Il piccone del regime* (Rome, 1985), 12.

29. Manacorda and Tamassia, *Il piccone del regime* (above, n. 28).

30. For the British and American Archaeological Society, see the *Journal of the British–American Society of Rome* 1885–1912. The Society was founded in 1865; Ashby, after a period as a member, was elected an honorary member in 1905; he lectured every year to the Society. The principal archive of the Society is housed in the British School at Rome. For the establishment of the shire societies, see Levine, *The Amateur and the Professional* (above, n. 14), 40ff.

31. Ashby, *Campagna*, 2.

32. Thomas Ashby, 'Scrittori contemporanei di cose romane: Rodolfo Lanciani', *Archivio della Reale Società Romana di Storia Patria* 51 (1928), 103–43.

33. Rodolfo Lanciani, 'Delle scoperte di antichità avvenute nelle fondazioni degli edifici per le Ferrovie di stato nella già Villa Patrizi in Via Nomentana', *Rivista Tecnica delle Ferrovie Italiane* 14 (1918), 3–36. See also Joanna Bird, Amanda Claridge, Oliver Gilkes and David Neal, 'Porta Pia: excavations and survey in an area of suburban Rome Part 1', *PBSR* 61 (1993), 51–133, esp. pp. 103–5.

34. Giuseppe Lugli, 'Thomas Ashby', *Bullettino della Commissione Archeologica Comunale di Roma* 59 (1931), 287–95, at p. 290.

35. Ashby, *Aqueducts*, 9.

36. Ashby, *Aqueducts*, 10.

37. Charles Dickens, *Pictures from Italy* (London, 1998), 148–9, originally published 1846.

38. Cf. Alistair Crawford, 'Robert Macpherson 1814–72, the foremost photographer of Rome', *PBSR* 67 (1999), 353–403.

39. Ashby, *Campagna*, 20.

40. Ashby, *Aqueducts*, 15–18.

41. Thomas Ashby, 'The classical topography of the Roman Campagna — part I', *Papers of the British School at Rome* 1 (1902), 125–281, at p. 127; note Lorenzo Quilici, *Collatia* (*Forma Italiae Regio I*, vol. X) (Rome, 1974), 15–26 on the history of research on the topography of the Roman Campagna, and also the observations about post-Ashby research in this region in David Whitehouse, 'Una postilla su 'l'archeologia del paessaggio italiano'', *Archeologia Medievale* 14 (1987), 547–50.

42. Lorenzo Quilici, while researching in the Archivio Centrale dello Stato, *Ministero della Pubblica Istruzione, Direzione Generale Antichità e Belle Arti*, vers. I, b.84, f. 232, April 1903, discovered that Ashby requested permission to excavate several villas, but his request was refused: 'La villa nel suburbio romano: problemi di studio e di inquadramento storico-topografico', *Archeologia Classica* 31 (1979), 309–17, at p. 309 (where Quilici mistakenly believed Ashby to be Director rather than Assistant Director at that time).

43. See Karin Einaudi (ed.), *Esther B. Van Deman* (Rome, 1991), especially pp. 7–23. Karin Einaudi recounted to me that the American archaeologist (and later director of the American Academy) Frank Brown, who as a young man had known both Ashby and Van Deman, found Van Deman to be a rather academic and severe person, not altogether likeable, whilst Ashby was charming and friendly (conversation on 26 January 1995).

44. E.M. Winslow, *A Libation to the Gods: the Story of the Roman Aqueducts* (London, 1963), xvi.

45. Einaudi, *Esther B. Van Deman* (above, n. 43), 21.

46. Einaudi, *Esther B. Van Deman* (above, n. 43), 23.

47. Einaudi, *Esther B. Van Deman* (above, n. 43), fig. 1, n. 1.

48. Ian Richmond, 'Review of Esther Boise Van Deman, *The Building of the Roman Aqueducts*', *Journal of Roman Studies* 26 (1936), 289–91, at p. 289.

49. Ashby, *Aqueducts*, x.

50. Richmond, 'Review of Van Deman, *The Building of the Roman Aqueducts*' (above, n. 48).

51. Ian Richmond, 'Editor's note', *Aqueducts*, vi.

52. Eric Birley, 'Sir Ian Archibald Richmond, 1902–1965', *Proceedings of the British Academy* 52 (1966), 293–302, at p. 295.

53. See, for example, the Italian edition edited by Giuseppina Pisani Sartorio, *Gli acquedotti dell'antica Roma* (Rome, 1991). Ashby clearly owed much to his collaborators and their work, but equally his collaborators also gained much from Ashby's knowledge: see the introduction by Vincenzo Reina, in V. Reina, G. Corbellini and G. Ducci, *Livellazione degli antichi acquedotti romani* (*Memorie della Società Italiane delle Scienze* 20) (Rome, 1917), 3–8, where he described how Ashby encouraged him to work on the engineering of the aqueducts.

54. R.V.D. Magoffin, 'Review of Thomas Ashby's *The Aqueducts of Ancient Rome*', *Journal of Roman Studies* 26 (1936), 287–8.

55. Cf. Graeme Barker, 'L'archeologia del paesaggio italiano: nuovi orientamenti e recenti esperienze', *Archeologia Medievale* 13 (1986), 7–30.

56. See J.F. Cherry, J.L. Davis and E. Mantzourani, *Landscape Archaeology as Long-Term History: Northern Keos and the Cycladic Islands* (Los Angeles, 1991); and the review of this book by A. Ammerman, *Journal of Field Archaeology* 20 (1993), 367–72.

57. For a definition of this method, expounded by a student of Lugli's, see Fernando Castagnoli, *Topografia di Roma antica* (Turin, 1980), 1–10.

58. Lorenzo Quilici, 'La Campagna romana come suburbio di Roma antica', *La Parola del Passato* 29 (1974), 410–38; Quilici, 'La villa nel suburbio romano' (above, n. 42).

59. Thomas Ashby, *Forty Drawings of Roman Scenes by British Artists (1715–1850) from Originals in the British Museum* (London, 1911).

60. Tomassetti, 1927: 81–105.

61. Didier Bodart, *Dessins de la collection Thomas Ashby à Bibliothèque Vaticane* (*Biblioteca Apostolica Vaticana, Documenti e riproduzioni* 2) (Vatican City, 1975); Raymond Keaveney (ed.), *Views of Rome. From the Thomas Ashby Collection in the Vatican Library* (London, 1988).

62. A.H. Smith, 'Memorandum for the Executive Sub-Committee', in the Executive Committee file for 1924.

63. Arnold Nesselrath, 'Codex Coner — 85 years on', in *Cassiano Dal Pozzo's Paper Museum* (*Quaderni Puteani* 3) (Ivrea, 1992), 145–68, at pp. 146 and 167.

64. Duncan Mackenzie, 'Dolmens and nuraghi of Sardinia', *PBSR* 6 (1913), 127–70, at p. 127.

65. Ashby may have been conscious not only of the energetic excavation programme of the British School at Athens (see H. Waterhouse, *The British School at Athens: the First Hundred Years* (London, 1986)), but also the likely failure to procure a permit to dig sites in the environs of Rome (see n. 42 above on his attempts to secure permission to excavate).

66. I owe this information to Dr Nicoletta Momigliano, who has studied the Arthur Evans's archive in the Ashmolean Museum; see her essay 'Duncan Mackenzie: a cautious canny highlander', in C. Morris (ed.), *Klados, Essays in Honour of J.N. Coldstream* (*Bulletin of the Institute of Classical Studies Supplement* 63) (London, 1995), 163–70; and *Duncan Mackenzie: a Cautious Canny Highlander and the Palace of Minos at Knossos* (London, 1999). Professor Colin Renfrew recollected meeting some of Mackenzie's workmen from Knossos (they had worked for Mackenzie as pot-boys): they spoke of his excellent Greek and his easy capacity to get on with peasants. Professor Renfrew considered Mackenzie's archaeological survey of Melos to be innovative for Greek archaeology in the 1890s. See also Joseph MacGillivray, *Minotaur. Sir Arthur Evans and the Archaeology of the Minoan Myth*

(London, 2000), especially pp. 171, 238–9 and 266–7, for interesting insights on Evans's relationship with Mackenzie.

67. Colin Renfrew and Malcolm Wagstaff (eds), *An Island Polity. The Archaeology of Exploitation in Melos* (Cambridge, 1982), 35–6; see n. 66 above.
68. *British School at Rome. Session 1905–6. Sixth Annual Report of the Managing Committee*, 5.
69. *British School at Rome. Twelfth Annual Report to the Subscribers 1911–1912*, 2.
70. Letter in the Ashby archive dated 29. v. '21; note Myres's comment referred to in T. Ashby, R.N. Bradley, T.E. Peet and N. Tagliaferro, 'Excavations in 1908–11 in various megalithic buildings in Malta and Gozo', *Papers of the British School at Rome* 6 (1913), 1–126, at p. 97, n. 1.
71. On Richard Colt Hoare's visit to Malta see John Evans, *The Prehistoric Antiquities of the Maltese Islands: a Survey* (London, 1971), 3. Ashby described his interest in Colt Hoare in *Campagna*, 175.
72. Ashby *et al.*, 'Excavations in 1908–11 in various megalithic buildings in Malta and Gozo' (above, n. 70), 2.
73. On Themistocles Zammit see John Evans, *Malta* (London, 1959), 23; Evans, *The Prehistoric Antiquities of the Maltese Islands* (above, n. 71), 3–4.
74. See, for example, J.N.L. Myres, *Dawn of History* (London, 1911).
75. Thomas Ashby, 'Supplementary excavations at Hal-Tarxien, Malta, in 1921', *Antiquaries Journal* 4 (new series) (1924), 93–100. See also above, n. 70.
76. Evans, *Malta* (above, n. 73), 52.
77. Thomas Ashby, 'Roman Malta', *Journal of Roman Studies* 5 (1914), 23–80, at p. 25.
78. Tomassetti, 1927: 78, n. 1.

TO CHAPTER THREE

1. This leaflet was issued by the Commissioners for the 1851 Exhibition, advertising the British School at Rome.
2. George M. Trevelyan, *Garibaldi's Defence of the Roman Republic* (London, 1910), 1; see also David Cannadine, *G.M. Trevelyan. A Life in History* (London, 1992), 88.
3. Cannadine, *G.M. Trevelyan* (above, n. 2), 66.
4. John Pemble, *The Mediterranean Passion. Victorians and Edwardians in the South* (Oxford, 1987), 81.
5. Quoted in Pemble, *The Mediterranean Passion* (above, n. 4), 81.
6. Quoted by Hugh Petter, *Lutyens in Italy* (London, 1992), 26.
7. Quoted in Wiseman, 1990: 1.
8. Quoted in Wiseman, 1990: 2.
9. T.P. Wiseman, 'Con Boni nel foro: i diari romani di W. St. Clair Baddeley', *Rivista dell'Istituto Nazionale di Archeologia e Storia dell'Arte* 8–9 (1985–6), 119–49.
10. Quoted in Wiseman, 1990: 3.
11. Francis Haverfield, 'Henry Francis Pelham, 1846–1907', *Proceedings of the British Academy* 3 (1907–8), 365–70, at p. 366.
12. T.P. Wiseman, 'The first Director of the British School', *PBSR* 49 (1981), 144–63, at pp. 146–7.
13. E.V. Lucas, *Two Englishwomen in Rome 1871–1900* (London, 1938), 226.
14. *British School at Rome. Report for the Session 1901–02*, 3.
15. Wiseman, 'First Director' (above, n. 12), 150.
16. *British School at Rome. Report for the Session 1902–03*, 1. As was noted in Chapter Two, Ashby was probably conscious of the importance of excavations to the fund-raising success (and academic status) of the rival British School at Athens, and in 1903 attempted to obtain permits for excavation of Roman villas in the Campagna Romana.
17. Wiseman, 1990: 6.
18. Virginia Woolf offers no comment upon the circumstances in her biography of this distinguished artist and critic: Virginia Woolf, *Roger Fry: a Biography* (New York/Toronto,

1940).

19.   *British School at Rome. Session 1905–6. Sixth Annual Report of the Managing Committee*, 3;
      F.H. Stubbings, 'Alan John Bayard Wace, 1879–1957', *Proceedings of the British Academy*
      44 (1958), 263–80, at pp. 266–7.
20.   Quoted in Wiseman, 1990: 6.
21.   *British School at Rome. Session 1906–7. Seventh Annual Report of the Managing Committee*,
      2.
22.   Thomas Ashby to Evelyn Shaw, 6 January 1918.
23.   Quoted in Wiseman, 1990: 8.
24.   *British School at Rome. Session 1908–9. Ninth Annual Report of the Managing Committee*, 2.
      See Mary Beard, *The Invention of Jane Harrison* (Cambridge (Mass.), 2000), 14–29 for an
      interesting account of Strong's early career and relationships.
25.   Lucas, *Two Englishwomen in Rome* (above, n. 13), 226.
26.   Gladys S. Thomson, *Mrs Arthur Strong. A Memoir* (London, 1949), 60.
27.   Barbara Tuchman, *The Proud Tower. A Portrait of the World before the War, 1890–1914*
      (London, 1980), 38.
28.   Quoted by Thomson, *Mrs Arthur Strong* (above, n. 26), 70–1.
29.   Quoted in Petter, *Lutyens in Italy* (above, n. 6), 14.
30.   Quoted in Petter, *Lutyens in Italy* (above, n. 6), 18.
31.   Quoted in Wiseman, 1990: 11.
32.   Quoted in Petter, *Lutyens in Italy* (above, n. 6), 29.
33.   Quoted in Petter, *Lutyens in Italy* (above, n. 6), 29–30.
34.   Petter, *Lutyens in Italy* (above, n. 6), 34–5.
35.   Eugénie Strong to Evelyn Shaw, 11 May 1914.
36.   The postcards are in the collection of Ashby and Eugénie Strong's postcards in the archives of
      the School.
37.   Evelyn Shaw was born in 1882 and educated at Trinity College, Oxford; he was Assistant
      Secretary of the Royal Commission of 1851 from 1904 to 1910, then Secretary from 1910 to
      1947. He was Honorary General Secretary to the British School at Rome from 1912 to 1947.
      On his retirement, he received a knighthood (*Who's Who*, 1972).
38.   Quoted in Petter, *Lutyens in Italy* (above, n. 6), 43.
39.   Eugénie Strong to Evelyn Shaw, 10 August 1917.
40.   Thomas Ashby to Evelyn Shaw, 11 January 1919.

TO CHAPTER FOUR

1.   In the box concerned with Ashby's service in the First World War, in the Ashby archive of the
      British School at Rome. The poem was written on the occasion of Ashby's birthday, eleven
      days before the beginning of the Caporetto offensive by the Germans.
2.   *The Record of the First British Red Cross Unit for Italy* (London, 1919) (hereafter cited as
      Record); David Cannadine, *G.M. Trevelyan. A Life in History* (London, 1992), 79–81.
3.   G.M. Trevelyan, *Garibaldi and the Making of Italy* (London, 1911), ix.
4.   Cannadine, *G.M. Trevelyan* (above, n. 2), 78.
5.   Cannadine, *G.M. Trevelyan* (above, n. 2), 80.
6.   Freya Stark, *Traveller's Prelude. Autobiography 1893–1927* (London, 1985), 180.
7.   Lynda Morris (ed.), *Henry Tonks and the 'Art of Pure Drawing'* (Norwich, 1985), 44,
      recorded that Tonks, then aged 53, considered that the Unit was badly organized and returned
      to London by November 1915; see also Joseph Hone, *The Life of Henry Tonks* (London,
      1939).
8.   Stark, *Traveller's Prelude* (above, n. 6), 187–9.
9.   Trevelyan, 'The work of the Unit', in *Record*, 14.
10.   Trevelyan, 'The work of the Unit', in *Record*, 15.
11.   Trevelyan, 'The work of the Unit', in *Record*, 17.
12.   Trevelyan, 'The work of the Unit', in *Record*, 18.

13. G.M. Trevelyan, cited in Smith, 1931: 523.
14. Lady Berwick, *The Times*, 20 May 1931.
15. 'Editorial', *Trento* 1 (4) (July 1916), 2.
16. Trevelyan, 'The work of the Unit', in *Record*, 26.
17. Logbook for car no. 95 (2/4/17 to 12/10/17) in the box-files concerned with Ashby's service in the First World War, British School at Rome archives.
18. Trevelyan, 'The work of the unit', in *Record*, 26.
19. Ernest Hemingway, *A Farewell to Arms* (Harmondsworth, 1935), especially pp. 15ff.
20. Stark, *Traveller's Prelude* (above, n. 6), 199.
21. G.M. Trevelyan, *Scenes from Italy's War* (London, 1919), 165–6.
22. Cyril Falls, *Caporetto 1917* (London, 1966); Hemingway, *A Farewell to Arms* (above, n. 19); see also Ben Pimlott, *Hugh Dalton* (London, 1985), 98–9.
23. Trevelyan, 'The work of the unit', in *Record*, 53.
24. *Villa Trento Circle of the British + Italian League. Unit Notes* I, May 1920, 5
25. *Villa Trento Circle of the British + Italian League. Unit Notes* II, July 1921, part ii, 2.
26. *Villa Trento Circle of the British + Italian League* III, 1922, 4.
27. Trevelyan, *Scenes from Italy's War* (above, n. 21).
28. I owe this information to Dr Philip Freeman who has been working on a study of Francis Haverfield; see also George MacDonald, 'Francis John Haverfield, 1860–1919', *Proceedings of the British Academy* 9 (1919), 475–91, at pp. 486–7.
29. Pimlott, *Hugh Dalton* (above, n. 22), 96.

TO CHAPTER FIVE

1. John Carswell, *Government and the Universities in Britain* (Cambridge, 1985), 3.
2. Frederick Kenyon, *The British Academy. The First Fifty Years* (London, 1952), 15, 31.
3. *Reports of the Executive Committee and Faculties*, 24 November 1920, 25 November 1931.
4. A.H. Smith, 'Memorandum for the Executive Sub-Committee', in the Executive Committee file for 1924.
5. 'Minutes of the Eighth Meeting of the Executive Committee. 30th May 1924', in the Executive Committee file for 1924.
6. Letter from John Forsdyke to Evelyn Shaw, 21 June 1924.
7. D. Kurtz (ed.), *Bernard Ashmole, 1894–1988. An Autobiography* (Oxford, 1994), 36.
8. The donation of his brick-stamp collection to the American Academy in Rome may be indicative of Ashby's well-concealed feelings for his own institution: James C. Anderson, *Roman Brickstamps: The Thomas Ashby Collection (Archaeological Monograph of the British School at Rome* 3) (London, 1991), 13. On Eugénie Strong's views see her letter to Evelyn Shaw, 20 June 1936.
9. See published writings, in *Bernard Ashmole* (above, n. 17), 191–4.
10. Two of these works are now in the Primary Collection of the National Portrait Gallery, London, although not on display at present (June 2000): 'Thomas Ashby', bronze head by David Evans, 1925, 406 mm high, NPG 4281; 'Thomas Ashby', pencil drawing by Sir George Clausen, 1925, 229 × 203 mm, NPG 3169.
11. Winifred Knights wrote as follows to her mother in an undated letter of August 1925: 'Great changes this summer. Ashby has left the school & is settled in his new flat. Mrs Strong has gone also to England & then back here to her flat. It was rather sad at the last to see them go & such young things are Ashmole & his young Librarian' — unpublished letter (LXXII) in the archive of the Strang Print Room, The Slade, University College, London.
12. Gladys S. Thomson, *Mrs Arthur Strong. A Memoir* (London, 1949), 94.
13. Bruno Bonelli in an interview with the author on 12 January 1995.
14. Kurtz, *Bernard Ashmole* (above, n. 7), 36–7.
15. Ralegh Radford in a letter to the author, 21 January 1994; note also E.A. Winslow's description in *A Libation to the Gods: the Story of the Roman Aqueducts* (London, 1963), xiii.
16. John Ward-Perkins, 'Introduction', in *Campagna*, x.

17. Giuseppe Lugli, 'Thomas Ashby', *Bullettino della Commissione Archeologica Comunale di Roma* 59 (1931), 292.

18. Giuseppe Lugli, 'Piccole avventure romane di un archeologo militante', *Strenna di Romanisti* 7 (1946), 49.

19. Thomas Ashby, 'Introduction', in W.J. Anderson and R.P. Spiers, *Architecture of Greece and Rome* (London, 1927), ix.

20. Thomas Ashby, *Some Italian Scenes and Festivals* (London, 1929,) viii; partly republished as *Sagre e feste d'Abruzzo* (Ortona, 1995) — see pp. 5–15, where Maria Concetta Nicolai has shown Ashby's interest in this subject to be part of a long British fascination for Abruzzese folkways and, more especially, to be a result of his friendship with the distinguished honorary inspector of antiquities in the Abruzzo, Antonio De Nino.

21. Mrs S.B. Platner to Thomas Ashby, once in the archives of the British School at Rome: quoted by Anderson, *Roman Brickstamps* (above, n. 8), 7. Alistair Crawford has suggested to me that this breakdown can be detected in the deteriorating quality of Ashby's photographs. The later photographs, unlike his early ones, show scant regard for composition.

22. Director's copy of *PBSR* 6 (1913).

23. See 'The British Academy of Arts in Rome', *Annales Institutorum* (1929–30), 51.

24. Tomassetti, 1927: 77.

25. D.H. Lawrence to A.W. McLeod, in Aldous Huxley (ed.), *The Letters of D.H. Lawrence* (London, 1932), 119–20.

26. J. Mulvaney, 'Another university man gone wrong', in D. Harris (ed.), *The Archaeology of V. Gordon Childe. Contemporary Perspectives* (London, 1994), 55–74, at pp. 67–8.

27. Thomas Ashby to a Mr Leslie, 20 June 1924, in the Miscellaneous Box 1 of the Ashby archive.

28. Thomson, *Mrs Arthur Strong* (above, n. 12), 98.

29. Eugénie Strong, 'La formazione delle accademie e scuole straniere di Roma', *Capitolium* May 1928.

30. The late Professor Krautheimer described his encounter with Ashby and Eugénie Strong to me during a dinner hosted by Karin Einaudi in January 1993.

31. Thomas Ashby, 'Scrittori contemporanei di cose romane: Rodolfo Lanciani', *Archivio della Reale Società Romana di Storia Patria* 51 (1928), 103–43.

32. Ian Richmond, 'Editor's note', *Aqueducts*, viii.

33. Richmond, 'Editor's note', *Aqueducts*, vi. Richmond noted in his report to the Faculty of Archaeology, History and Letters for 1931 (*Reports of the Executive Committee and Faculties*, 25 November, 1931, 12):

> The writer would wish to put on record not only the many kindnesses and invaluable help which he received as a pupil from Dr. Ashby, but the unswerving friendship which continued until his last journey towards England, when he and Dr. Ashby worked together in April at Spello. This was to have been the beginning of a fruitful partnership, had not *atrox fortuna* snatched him too early from the science he loved so well.

Ashby, it seems, following the completion of *Aqueducts*, was embarking on a new project with Richmond, focused on the Roman town of Spello (Umbria).

34. *Aqueducts*, v; note, however, Winslow's account of meeting Ashby in April 1931, in which he portrayed him as an ebullient, if slightly eccentric, man: Winslow, *A Libation to the Gods* (above, n. 15).

35. Ralegh Radford in a letter to the author, 21 January 1994.

36. Lord Stanley, now chairman of the Executive Committee.

37. Ian Richmond was now the Director of the British School at Rome.

38. This was eventually published as (Smith, 1931: 525):

> The first appointment to the Directorship of the Incorporated School dated, as already said, from June 1912, and then and thereafter was made for successive terms of three years. The question of renewal in 1924 came up for examination in June of that year, and Ashby was informed that the Executive Council had decided to renew the

appointment for one year only, until 30 June 1925. The action of the Committee, as stated at the time, related solely to matters of internal administrative policy, and it was with a very real sense of regret that they finally terminated the appointment of one who had rendered such conspicuous service to the School.

Though the notification came as a surprise and disappointment to Ashby, he nevertheless accepted it in that spirit of unquestioning loyalty which was always one of the finest traits in his character.

39. See Kurtz, *Bernard Ashmole* (above, n. 7), 46–7.
40. See Alan Sorrell, *Barbarians in Rome*, unpublished manuscript, pp. 95–6 (cited in Wiseman, 1990: 16) for a vivid account of Smith's Directorship.
41. Eric Birley, 'Sir Ian Archibald Richmond, 1902–1965', *Proceedings of the British Academy* 52 (1966), 293–302.
42. See *Reports of the Executive Committee and Faculties*, 25 November 1931, 3–4, and 12 which describes how Mr William Russell, the Honorary Treasurer of the Faculty of Archaeology, History and Letters, assisted with the acquisition of Ashby's library. The *Reports of the Executive Committee and Faculties* April 1934 suggest that the library was purchased for £2,000. Note also the following document in the School's archives: *Library of the late Dr. Thomas Ashby*. (1) Memorandum of sale of library to B.S.R. 2/10/31; (2) Memmorandum [sic] of loan of Manuscript and print collection to Mr. Richmond 3/10/31.
43. Colin Hardie in an interview with the author on 19 July 1992; see Leonard Boyle, in R. Keaveney (ed.), *Views of Rome. From the Thomas Ashby Collection in the Vatican Library* (London, 1988), 18–19.

TO CHAPTER SIX

1.   I owe this reference to David Bass. 'I thought I heard the voice of my old producer: 'What! It finishes like that ... without a gleam of hope, a ray of sunshine? At least give me a ray of sunshine', he begged me at the first showings of my films ... A ray of sunshine? Well, I don't know, let's try.'
2.   Giuseppe Lugli, 'Piccole avventure romane di un archeologo militante', *Strenna di Romanisti* 7 (1946), 42–50.
3.   See Lorenzo Quilici, *Collatia (Forma Italiae Regio I* vol. X) (Rome, 1974), 25.
4.   John Ward-Perkins, 'Notes on Southern Etruria and the Ager Veientanus', *PBSR* 23 (1955), 44–72, at p. 44; see John Wilkes, 'John Bryan Ward-Perkins, 1912–1981', *Proceedings of the British Academy* 69 (1981), 631–55.
5.   Graeme Barker, 'L'archeologia del paesaggio italiano: nuovi orientamenti e recenti esperienze', *Archeologia Medievale* 13 (1986), 7–30; cf. Stefania Quilici Gigli, 'The changing landscape of the Roman Campagna', in J. Carlsen (ed.), *Landuse in the Roman Empire (Analecta Romana Instituti Danici Supplementum XXII)* (Rome 1994), 135–43.
6.   David Whitehouse, 'Una postilla su 'L'archeologia del paesaggio italiano'', *Archeologia Medievale* 14 (1987), 547–50.
7.   Accompanied by a substantial catalogue: *Thomas Ashby: un archeologo fotografa la Campagna Romana fra '800 e '900* (Rome, 1986).
8.   Catalogue: *Archeologia a Roma nelle fotografie di Thomas Ashby 1891–1930* (Naples, 1989).
9.   Catalogue: *Il Lazio di Thomas Ashby 1891–1930* (Rome, 1994).
10. Raymond Keaveney (ed.), *Views of Rome. From the Thomas Ashby Collection in the Vatican Library* (London, 1988).
11. Thomas Ashby, *Gli acquedotti dell'antica Roma* (edited by Giuseppina Pisani Sartorio) (Rome, 1991).
12. Arnold Nesselrath, 'Codex Coner — 85 years on', *The Paper Museum of Cassiano Dal Pozzo (Quaderni Puteani* 3) (Ivrea, 1992), 145–68. More recently see, for example, John Osborne and Amanda Claridge, *Early Christian and Medieval Antiquities (Catalogue Raisonné of the Paper Museum of Cassiano dal Pozzo. Series A. Antiquities and Architecture)* 1. *Mosaics and*

Wall Paintings in Rome (London, 1996); 2. *Other Mosaics, Paintings, Sarcophagi and Small Objects* (London, 1998).

13. George Boon, 'Archaeology through the Severn Tunnel: the Caerwent Exploration Fund, 1899–1917', *Transactions of the Bristol and Gloucestershire Archaeological Society* 107 (1989), 5–26. See also Chapter Two, n. 26.

14. Eva Tea, *Giacomo Boni nella vita del suo tempo* (Milan, 1932).

15. Tomassetti, 1927.

16. Norma Clarke, 'Strenous idleness. Thomas Carlyle and the man of letters as hero', in M. Roper and J. Tosh (eds), *Manful Assertions. Masculinities in Britain since 1800* (London, 1991), 25–43, at p. 39.

17. Thomas Ashby, *Turner's Visions of Rome* (London, 1924), 19–20.

18. D. Kurtz (ed.), *Bernard Ashmole, 1894–1988. An Autobiography* (Oxford, 1994), 28.

19. Gladys S. Thomson, *Mrs Arthur Strong. A Memoir* (London, 1949), 100. On the place of women and wives within archaeological contexts at this time see J.P. Droop, *Archaeological Excavations* (Cambridge, 1915), 63–4:

> of a mixed dig however I have seen something, and it is an experiment that I would be reluctant to try again. I would grant if need be that women are admirably fitted for the work, yet I would uphold that they should undertake it by themselves ... mixed digging means a loss of easiness in the atmosphere and consequently loss of efficiency. A minor, and yet to my mind weighty, objection lies in one particular form of constraint entailed by the presence of ladies, it must add to all the strains of an excavation, and they are many, the further strain of politeness and self-restraint in moments of stress, moments that will occur on the best regulated dig, when you want to say what you think without translation, which before ladies, whatever their feelings about it, cannot be done.

See also P.R.S. Moorey, 'British women in Near Eastern archaeology. Kathleen Kenyon and the pioneers', *Palestine Exploration Quarterly* 124 (1992), 91–100, especially pp. 92–3.

20. J.B. Priestley, *English Journey* (London, 1934), 397–401.

21. Alan Bennett, *Writing Home* (London, 1994), 119.

22. Lugli, 'Piccole avventure romane di un archeologo militante' (above, n. 2), 42.

APPENDIX

SELECTED BIBLIOGRAPHY

SELECTED WORKS BY THOMAS ASHBY — excluding book reviews
(* — referred to in text)

1898
*Sul vero sito del Lago Regillo. *Rendiconti della Classe di Scienze Morali, Storiche e Filologiche dell'Accademia dei Lincei, Roma* serie V, 7: 103–26.
The true site of Lake Regillus. *Classical Review* 12: 470–2.

1899
Recent excavations in Rome. *Classical Review* 13: 184–6, 232–5, 321–2, 464–7.

1900
*The four great aqueducts of Ancient Rome. *Classical Review* 14: 325–7.
Recent excavations in Rome. *Classical Review* 14: 236–40.
Termine forse miliario scoperto al XIII miglio della Via Prenestina. *Rendiconti della Classe di Scienze Morali, Storiche e Filologiche dell'Accademia dei Lincei, Roma* serie V, 9: 217–19.
*Un altro panorama di Roma delineato da Antonio Van Den Wyngaerde. *Bullettino della Commissione Archeologica Comunale di Roma* 28: 28–32.

1900–1
The collegia of ancient Rome. *Journal of the British and American Archaeological Society of Rome* 3: 101–11.

1901
*(with A.T. Martin and A.E. Hudd) Excavations at Caerwent, Monmouthshire, on the site of the Roman city of Venta Silurum, in 1899 and 1900. *Archaeologia* 57: 295–316.
*Un panorama de Rome par Antoine Van Den Wyngaerde. *Mélanges d'Archéologie et d'Histoire de l'École Française de Rome* 21: 471–86.
Recent excavations in Rome. *Classical Review* 15: 85–9, 136–42, 328–30.
*The true site of Alba Longa. *Journal of Philology* 27: 37–50.

1901–2
The Campagna in ancient times. *Journal of the British and American Archaeological Society of Rome* 3: 139–44.

1902
*Classical topography of the Roman Campagna. — I. *PBSR* 1: 125–285.
*(with A.E. Hudd and A.T. Martin) Excavations at Caerwent, Monmouthshire, on the site of the Romano-British city of Venta Silurum, in 1901. *Archaeologia* 58: 119–52.
Recent excavations in Rome. *Classical Review* 16: 94–6, 284–6.

1903

Archaeological notes from Rome. *Pilot* 466ff.

*Dessins inédits de Carlo Labruzzi. *Mélanges d'Archeologie et d'Histoire de l'École Française de Rome* 23: 375–418.

*(with A.E. Hudd and A.T. Martin) Excavations at Caerwent, Monmouthshire, on the site of the Romano-British city of Venta Silurum, in 1902. *Archaeologia* 58: 391–46.

Recent excavations in Rome. *Classical Review* 17: 135–7, 328–9.

1903–4

Roman villas in the Campagna. *Journal of the British and American Archaeological Society of Rome* 3: 258–63.

1904

The acqueducts of ancient Rome. *Public Works* 2 (3): 193–201.

Documenti inediti relativi alla storia della Via Appia. In *Atti del congresso internazionale di scienze storiche* 5: 125–33.

*(with A.E. Hudd and A.T. Martin) Excavations at Caerwent, Monmouthshire, on the site of the Romano-British city of Venta Silurum, in the years 1901–1903. *Archaeologia* 59: 87–124.

Excavations at Caerwent, Monmouthshire. *Man* 4: 101–7

The public baths of ancient Rome. *Public Works* 4 (4): 320–30.

Recent discoveries in the Roman Forum. *Builder* 87: 88, 692.

Recent excavations in Rome. *Classical Review* 18: 137–41, 328–31.

The recent excavations in the Forum romanum 1898–1903. *Builder* 86: 2–4, 574–5.

Roman drainage works and rivers regulations. *Public Works* 2 (4): 306–14.

Roman notes. *Builder* 87: 178.

*Sixteenth-century drawings of Roman buildings attributed to Andreas Coner. *PBSR* 2 (whole volume).

Some account of a volume of epigraphic drawings now preserved in the British Museum. *Classical Review* 18: 70–5.

1904–5

Renaissance plans and drawings of Rome. *Journal of the British and American Archaeological Society of Rome* 3: 333–7.

1905

Ancient Abruzzese art at Chieti. *Builder* 89: 667.

(with G.J. Pfeiffer) Carseoli: a description of the site and the Roman remains, with historical notes and a bibliography. *Supplementary Papers of the American School in Rome* 1: 108–40.

Il Circeo. *Mélanges d'Archéologie et d'Histoire de l'École Française de Rome* 25: 157–209.

(with G.J. Pfeiffer) La Civita near Artena in the province of Rome. *Supplementary Papers of the American School in Rome* 1: 87–107.

*Excavations at Caerwent, Monmouthshire, on the site of the Romano-British city of Venta Silurum, in the year 1904. *Archaeologia* 59: 289–301.

Recent excavations in Rome. *Classical Review* 19: 74–9, 328–30.

Recent discoveries in Rome. *Builder* 89: 693–4.

Recent discoveries on the Caelian Hill, Rome. *Builder* 89: 7–8.

Roman villas in the Campagna di Roma. *Builder* 89: 317.

The so called Temple of Minerva Medica. *Builder* 88: 520–31.

1905–6

The site of Gabii. *Journal of the British and American Archaeological Society of Rome*
  3: 484.
The British School at Rome. *Classical Review* 19: 183–4.

1906

*Another panorama of Rome by Anton Van Den Wyngaerde. *Mélanges d'Archéologie et
  d'Histoire de l'École Française de Rome* 26: 179–93.
The British School at Rome. *Classical Review* 20: 235–6.
*The classical topography of the Roman Campagna. — II. *PBSR* 3: 1–212.
*Excavations at Caerwent, Monmouthshire, on the site of the Romano-British city of
  Venta Silurum, in the year 1905. *Archaeologia* 60: 111–30.
The Forum of Trajan and other notes from Rome. *Builder* 91: 679–80.
Italian excavations. *Year's Work in Classical Studies*: 9–15.
Notes from Rome. *Builder* 90: 579–80.
Places of public resort in ancient Rome. *Public Works* 7 (1): 1–7.
Recent excavations in Rome. *Classical Review* 20: 132–6, 378–80.
The Via Cavour and the Imperial Fora in Rome. *Builder* 91: 166–7.

1906–7

*The Via Latina. *Journal of the British and American Archaeological Society of Rome* 4
  (30–1): 30–2.

1907

Ancient remains near the Via Clodia. *Mitteilungen des Deutschen Archäologischen
  Instituts, Römische Abteilung* 22: 311–32.
*The classical topography of the Roman Campagna, Part III, Section I. *PBSR* 4: 1–159.
*Excavations at Caerwent, Monmouthshire, on the site of the Romano-British city of
  Venta Silurum, in the year 1906. *Archaeologia* 60: 451–64.
Herculaneum. *Independent* 4 July: 21–5.
Italian excavations. *Year's Work in Classical Studies*: 18–26.
Notes from Rome. *Builder* 92: 315–16.
*Prehistoric monuments of Sardinia. *Builder* 91: 589, 592.
Recent archaeological research in Italy. *Times* 27 December.

1908

The aqueducts of ancient Rome. *Builder* 94: 37ff., 64, 89ff., 111ff., 142, 174ff., 203ff.,
  234ff.
Ausonia. *Journal of Hellenic Studies* 28: 165.
Italian excavations. *Year's Work in Classical Studies*: 21–30.
Recent archaeological research in Italy. *Times* 31 December 1908.
Recent excavations in Rome. *Classical Quarterly* 2: 142–50.
The rediscovery of Rome. *Quarterly Review* 416: 101–22.
The traffic and housing problem in Rome. *Builder* 95: 665ff.
An unknown sixteenth century topography of Rome. *Archaeological Journal* 65: 245–64.
The Villa d'Este at Tivoli and the collection of classical sculptures which it contained.
  Archaeologia 61: 219–56.
The villa of the Quintilii. *Builder* 94: 174.

1908–9

Recent excavations at Caerwent. *Journal of the British and American Archaeological Society* 4: 284–6.

1909

The ancient aqueducts of Lyon. *Builder* 96: 357.

Die antiken Wasserleitungen der Stadt Rom. *Neue Jahrbücher für das Klassische Altertum, Geschichte und Deutsche Literatur* 23: 246–60.

Destruction of ancient monuments. *Journal of the Royal Society of Antiquaries of Ireland* 39: 203.

*(with A.E. Hudd and F. King) Excavations at Caerwent, Monmouthshire, on the site of the Romano-British city of Venta Silurum, in the years 1907 and 1909. *Archaeologia* 61: 565–82.

Ferentinum. *Mitteilungen des Deutschen Archäologischen Instituts, Römische Abteilung* 24: 1–58.

An important inscription relating to the Social War. *Classical Review* 22 (5): 158–9.

Italian excavations. *Year's Work in Classical Studies*: 19–33.

*The Latin shore. *Independent* October 28: 969–76.

Old and new Rome. *Builder* 97: 87–9.

Prehistoric antiquities of Malta. *Builder* 96: 433.

Recent excavations in Malta. *Builder* 96: 59.

Gli scavi di Caerwent, Inghilterra. *Studi Storici per l'Antichità Classica* 2 (1): 52–62.

Some recent discoveries in Rome and Ostia. *Builder* 96: 265–6.

La villa dei Quintilii. *Ausonia. Rivista della Società Italiana di Archeologia e Storia dell'Arte* 4 (1): 48–88.

1909–10

The 'Campagna di Roma'. *Journal of the British and American Archaeological Society* 4: 316–31.

Casts at the British Museum; Sarcophagus of Alexander Severus. *Journal of the Royal Institute of British Architects* ser. 3 17: 88ff.

1910

Ancora sugli affreschi di Perino del Vaga provenienti da Palazzo Baldassini. *Bollettino d'Arte* 4 (1): 68.

The battle of Lake Trasimene. *Journal of Philology* 31: 117–22.

*The classical topography of the Roman Campagna. — III. (The Via Latina) — Section II. *PBSR* 5: 213–432.

(with F.G. Newton) The Columbarium of Pomponius Hylas. *PBSR* 5: 461–71.

*(with A.E. Hudd and F. King) Excavations at Caerwent, Monmouthshire, on the site of the Romano-British city of Venta Silurum, in the year 1908. *Archaeologia* 62: 1–20.

Italian excavations. *Year's Work in Classical Studies*: 13–29.

The passeggiata archeologica or zona monumentale at Rome. *Builder* 98: 702.

Recent archaeological research in Italy. *Times* 6 March.

Topography of Rome. In J.E. Sandys (ed.), *A Companion to Latin Studies*: 35–47. Cambridge, Cambridge University Press.

1911

Archaeological restorations by French architects. *Builder* 101: 303–5.

The exhibitions at Rome in 1911. *Builder* 100: 617–19, 755; 101: 76–7.

*(with A.E. Hudd and F. King) Excavations at Caerwent, Monmouthshire, on the site of the Romano-British city of Venta Silurum, in the years 1909 and 1910. *Archaeologia* 62: 405–48.

Forty Drawings of Roman Scenes by British Artists (1715–1850) from Originals in the British Museum Prepared for the Commemorative Exhibition at Rome, 1911. London, British Museum.

British historical section. *Report of H.M.'s Commissioners on Brussels, Rome and Turin Exhibitions*: 116–22. London.

Italian excavations. *Year's Work in Classical Studies*: 9–20.

Lampedusa, Lampione and Linosa. *Annals of Archaeology and Anthropology (Liverpool)* 4: 11–34.

Malta. *Times* 4 August.

Malta. *Morning Post* 4 August.

Primitive burial in Malta. *Times* 13 May.

Primitive burial in Malta. *Daily Malta Chronicle* 22 May.

Publications relating to the papal collection in Rome. *Builder* 101: 297–300.

Recent discoveries in Rome. *Builder* 100: 487.

A Roman villa near Henley. *Archaeological Journal* 68 (269): 43–8.

Rome International Fine Arts Exhibition 1911: Souvenir of British Historical Section: 484–530, 650–6. London.

Rome. In *Transactions of the Town Planning Conference, London 10–15 October 1910*: 133–45. London, Royal Institute of British Architects.

1911–12

Encyclopaedia Britannica (all articles on the topography and geography of Italy (excluding Rome), and supplementary information in the *Yearbook* for 1912). (Includes entries for: Anagnia, Anzio, Caere, Circeo, Cori, Nemorensis Lacus, Norba, Praeneste, Setia, Signia, Tarquinii.)

The later Stuarts in Rome, 1719–1740. *Journal of the British and American Archaeological Society of Rome* 4: 624–33.

1912

*Appunti sulla Via Salaria. *Mitteilungen des Deutschen Archäologischen Instituts, Römische Abteilung* 27: 222–9.

The Archaeological Congress and the Congress of the History of Art in Rome, October 1912. *Builder* 103: 566.

Historical importance of Pompeii. *Nash's Magazine* September: 707.

Italian excavations. *Year's Work in Classical Studies*: 9–20.

Recent archaeological research in Italy. *Times* 4 January, 26 and 27 December.

Recent discoveries at Ostia. *Journal of Roman Studies* 2: 153–94.

Recent excavations at Rome and Pompeii. *Builder* 103: 375–6.

Rome (city of). *Harmsworth Encyclopaedia*. London.

Studi romani. *Journal of Roman Studies* 2: 280.

1913

*Addenda and corrigenda to *Sixteenth-century drawings of Roman buildings attributed to Andreas Coner (Papers of the British School at Rome, Vol. II.)*. *PBSR* 6: 184–210.

*The Alban Hills. *Quarterly Review* 435: 330–52.

*(with R.N. Bradley, T.E. Peet and N. Tagliaferro) Excavations in 1908–11 in the various Megalithic buildings in Malta and Gozo. *PBSR* 6: 1–126.

*Introduction. In M.H.U. Hogarth, *The Fountains of Rome*. Oxford.
*Italian excavations. *Year's Work in Classical Studies*: 21–30.
Maltese prehistoric remains. *Daily Malta Chronicle* April (special number): 12ff.
*Note to 'Roman remains in the town and territory of Velletri' by A. Pelzer Wagener. *American Journal of Archaeology* series II, 17: 399–428.
*Thomas Jenkins in Rome. *PBSR* 6: 487–511.
*Two Roman bridges in southern Etruria. *Builder* 105: 336.

1914

Archaeological research in Italy. *Times* 10 and 11 February.
La campagna romana al tempo di Paolo III. Mappa della Campagna romana di Eufrosino della Volpaia. Rome, Danesi.
*Drawings of ancient paintings in English collections. part I. — The Eton drawings. *PBSR* 7: 1–62.
(with G.H. Hallam) Horace's villa at Tivoli. *Journal of Roman Studies* 4: 121–38.
Italian excavations. *Year's Work in Classical Studies*: 11–20.
Notes to 'Civita Lavinia, the site of Ancient Lanuvium', by G.B. Colburn. *American Journal of Archaeology* 18: 185–98, 363–80.
Recent discoveries at Ostia. *Architectural Review* 45: 121–3, 142ff.
The recent excavations on the Palatine: discovery of the Mundus. *Times* 8 January.
Retracing Roman highways. *Argus* (Melbourne) 3 October: 4.
Un tableau de Jules Romain. *Revue Archéologique* 4, 24: 139.
*Turner in Rome. *Burlington Magazine* 24 (no. 130): 218–24; 25 (124): 98–104.
*Turner at Tivoli. *Burlington Magazine* 25 (no. 136): 241–7.

1914–15

Le diverse edizioni dei 'Vestigi dell'antichitá di Roma' di Stefano du Pérac. *Bibliofilia* 16: 401–21.
Il libro di Antonio Labacco appartenente all'architettura. *Bibliofilia* 16: 289–309.

1915

Archaeological investigations in Malta. Xrobb il Ghargin. *Proceedings of the British Association. Manchester Meeting*: 208–13. London.
Archaeological research in Italy. *Times Literary Supplement* 4 March: 75ff.
Italian excavations. *Year's Work in Classical Studies*: 1–8.
*Roman Malta. *Journal of Roman Studies* 5: 23–80.

1915–16

Le diverse edizioni dei 'Vestigi dell'antichitá di Roma' di Stefano du Pérac. *Bibliofilia* 17: 358–9.

1916

Archaeological research in Italy. *Times Literary Supplement* 11 May: 225.
*Drawings of ancient paintings in English collections. Part II. — The Holkham drawings. Part III. — The Baddeley codex. Part IV. — The Chatsworth sketch-book. *PBSR* 8: 35–54.
(with T. Zammit and G. Despott) Excavations in Malta in 1914. *Man* 16: nos. 1 and 14.
*The Palazzo Odescalchi in Rome. *PBSR* 8: 55–90.
Topographical Study in Rome in 1581. A Series of Views with a Fragmentary Text by

Etienne Du Pérac in the Library of C.W. Dyson Perrins Esq. London, J.B. Nichols and Sons.
*(with R. Gardner) The Via Traiana. *PBSR* 8: 104–71.

1916–17
*Le Vie Appia e Traiana. *Bollettino dell'Associazione Archeologica Romana* 6–7: 10–23.

1918
Un'altra pianta di Roma di Giovanni Battista Falda. *Rendiconti. Atti dell'Accademia Nazionale dei Lincei* serie V, 27: 235–6.
*Monsieur Henri Focillon's works on Piranesi. *Burlington Magazine* 33 (no. 188): 186–90.
Some festivals in the Abruzzi. *Anglo-Italian Review* 2: 308–19.

1919
(with R. Gardner) An ancient hill fortress in Lucania. *Journal of Roman Studies* 9: 211–15.
*The Bodleian Ms. of Pirro Ligorio. *Journal of Roman Studies* 9: 170–201.
Cipollino marble. *Builder* 117: 83.
Mr Walcot's etchings of Rome (the so called Stadium of Domitian and the Frigidarium of the Baths of Caracalla. *Architectural Review* 46: 79–81.
The so-called Stadium of Domitian and the Caracalla frigidarium. In *Architectural Water-Colours and Etchings of W. Walcot*: 31–7. London, Dickins.
Some festivals in the Abruzzi. *Anglo-Italian Review* 3: 45–51.

1920
*Antiquae Statuae Urbis Romae. *PBSR* 9: 107–58.
Archaeological research in Italy. *Times Literary Supplement* 15 January: 33; 22 January: 50; 2 December: 794; 16 December: 846.
Carteggio relativo all'origine dell'Instituto di Corrispondenza Archeologica conservato ora nell'Archivio di Stato. *Rendiconti. Atti dell'Accademia Nazionale dei Lincei* serie V, 29: 299–303.
Italian excavations. *Year's Work in Classical Studies*: 83–96.
*The Palazzo Odescalchi. *PBSR* 9: 67–74.

1920–1
La prima edizione dell''Urbis Romae Sciographia' di Stefano di Pérac. *Bibliofilia* 22: 357–8.
Treasures of the R.I.B.A. Library. *Journal of the Institute of British Architects* ser. 3 28: 171.

1921
The aqueducts of ancient Rome. *Illustrated London News* 9 July: 46ff.
Recent archaeological work in Italy. *Antiquaries Journal* 1: 61–3.
Recent excavations in Italy. *Times Literary Supplement* 15 December: 842; 21 December: 858.
The Sanudo diaries. *Times Literary Supplement* 13 January: 28.
*(with R.A.L. Fell) The Via Flaminia. *Journal of Roman Studies* 11: 125–90.
La villa d'Orazio a Tivoli. *Atti e Memorie della Società Tiburtina di Storia e d'Arte* 1: 3–29.

1922
Digging the treasure. Laden soil of Italy: a pre-Julian Roman calendar from Nero's villa. *Illustrated London News* 28 January: 110.

Measuring the miles from the city. *Morning Post* 5 February.
On the need for an index of measured drawings. *Architectural Association Journal* 37: 193.
Prehistoric Malta. *Illustrated London News* 25 February: 262ff.
Il promontorio Circeo e la città di Circeii: la città di Circeii sul lago di Paola. *Il Circeo* 11 February.
Il promontorio Circeo e la città di Circeii: il Monte Circeo. *Il Circeo* 14 January.
Recent archaeological work in Italy. *Antiquaries Journal* 2: 65–7.
Recent discoveries in Rome. *Illustrated London News* 28 January: 110ff.
Recent excavations in Italy. *Times Literary Supplement* 21 December: 858.
Recent excavations in Rome. *Journal of the Royal Institute of British Architects* 29: 553–67.
Some new Piranesi drawings. *Architectural Review* 51: 61.
*Turner ed i suoi predecessori a Roma. In *Atti del X Congresso internazionale di storia dell'arte in Roma. L'Italia e l'arte straniera*: 438–40. Rome, Maglioni e Strini.
*La Via Tiburtina. *Atti e Memorie della Società Tiburtina di Storia e d'Arte* 2: 74–88.

1922–3
Italian excavations. *Year's Work in Classical Studies*: 97–116.
La 'Roma antica' di Alò Giovannoli. *Bibliofilia* 24: 101–13.

1923
*Applicazione della fotografia aerea agli studi archeologici. *Reale Accademia Nazionale dei Lincei* 32: 186–7.
*Applicazione della fotografia aerea agli studi archeologici. *Bollettino dell'Associazione Archeologica Romana* 14: 3.
The Castra Peregrinorum. Compiled by P.K. Baillie Reynolds from notes made by T. Ashby. *Journal of Roman Studies* 13: 152–67.
*Lievin Cruyl e le sue vedute di Roma (1644–1670). *Memorie. Atti della Pontificia Accademia Romana di Archeologia* 1 (1): 221–9.
Note sulle varie guide di Roma che contengono zilografie di Girolamo Franzini. *Roma* 1 (9–10): 345–52.
A prehistoric capital (Les Eyzies, Dordogne, France). *Times* 28 September: 13.
A proposed historical atlas for Italy. *Saturday Review* 136 (14 July): 38ff.
Recent archaeological work in Italy. *Antiquaries Journal* 3: 158–60.
Rome. *Town Planning Review* 1: 43–52.
The Vasari Society. *Burlington Magazine* 42 (no. 239): 107.
*La Via Tiburtina. *Atti e Memorie della Società Tiburtina di Storia e d'Arte* 3: 3–35, 87–107.

1923–4
Hadrian's Villa at Tivoli. *Wonders of the Past* 19: 937–47.
The history of Palazzola. *Venerabile* 1: 289–97.
Italian excavations. *Year's Work in Classical Studies*: 105–19.
Nero's Golden House at Rome. *Wonders of the Past* 22: 1,138–44.
Ostia: port of ancient Rome. *Wonders of the Past* 17: 836–54.
Pirro Ligorio. *Journal of the Royal Institute of British Architects* 31: 153–4.
La prima edizione dei 'Vestigi di Roma' di Stefano Du Pérac. *Bibliofilia* 25: 191–2.
Recent excavations in Rome. *Journal of the Royal Institute of British Architects* 31: 553–71.

1924
Ancient Roman funerary art: notable new discoveries. *Illustrated London News* 5 April: 602–5.

*Due vedute di Roma attribuite a Stefano Du Pérac. In *Miscellanea Francesco Ehrle (Studi e Testi* 38) 2: 449–59.

The forum. *Illustrated London News* 14 June: 1,114ff.

New treasures from Italy's classic soil. *Illustrated London News* 12 April: 642–5.

Nuove note su varie guide di Roma. *Roma* 2: 201–9.

(with S.R. Pierce) The Piazza del Popolo: Rome. Its history and development. *Town Planning Review* 11 (2): 75–96.

Recent archaeological work in Italy. *Antiquaries Journal* 4: 263–5.

Recent excavations in Italy. *Times Literary Supplement* 10 January: 22; 17 January: 38.

Roman waters. *Times* 1 April.

*Supplementary excavations at Hal-Tarxien, Malta, in 1921. *Antiquaries Journal* 4 (new series): 93–100.

Topographical notes on Cozens. *Burlington Magazine* 45 (no. 259): 193ff.

*La Via Tiberina e i territori di Capena e del Soratte nel periodo romano. *Memorie della Pontificia Accademia* 1 (2): 129–75.

*La Via Tiburtina. *Atti e Memorie della Società Tiburtina di Storia e d'Arte* 4: 3–30, 107–36.

(with T.E. Peet and E. Thurlow Leeds) The Western Mediterranean. *Cambridge Ancient History*: 563–601. Cambridge, Cambridge University Press.

Where the Roman followers of a sect worshipped. *Sphere* 31 May: 242–3.

1924–5

The history of Palazzola. *Venerabile* 2: 3–13, 229ff.

Italian excavations. *Year's Work in Classical Studies*: 83–97.

A tradition regarding the foundation of the English Hospices in Rome. *Venerabile* 2: 240–4.

1925

Camillo Porcari (?–1521). *Rendiconti. Atti dell'Accademia Nazionale dei Lincei* serie VI, 1: 491–503.

*(with W.G. Constable) Canaletto and Bellotto in Rome. *Burlington Magazine* 46 (no. 266): 207–14; (no. 268): 288–99.

Frammenti di due piante ignote di Roma del secolo XVII. *Roma* 3 (7): 314–17.

Note sulle 'cose meravigliose'. *Roma* 3: 38–9.

Practical engineering in ancient Rome. In *Proceedings of the British Association for the Advancement of Science. Presidential Address to Section H (Anthropology). Southampton Meeting*: 134–55.

Practical engineering in ancient Rome. *Engineering* 120: 491–3, 527–8, 560–1.

Practical engineering in ancient Rome. *Nature* 116: 576–80.

A proposito di due frammenti inediti di due piante di Roma del sec. XVII. *Roma* 3: 422–3.

Recent archaeological work in Italy. *Antiquaries Journal* 5: 437–9.

Recent excavations in Italy. *Times Literary Supplement* 8 January: 22; 15 January: 38.

*Turner ed i suoi predecessori a Roma. In *L'Italia e l'arte straniera (Atti del X congresso internazionale di storia dell'arte in Roma)*: 438–40. Rome.

*Turner's Visions of Rome. London/New York, Halton and Truscott Smith Ltd.

1925–6

Impiego degli stessi rami per opere diverse in alcune edizioni romane. *La Bibliofilia* 27: 160–2.

Italian excavations. *Year's Work in Classical Studies*: 111–25.

1926

*Un geologo inglese in Italia alla fine del settecento (Frederick Harvey, Earl of Bristol, Bishop of Derry). *Atti e Memorie della Reale Accademia di Scienze, Lettere ed Arti di Padova* 42: 3–8.

The museum of the Roman empire in Rome. *Journal of Roman Studies* 16: 282–3.

Recent excavations in Italy. *Times Literary Supplement* 18 February.

S. Matteo in Merulana. *Roma* 4: 72.

1926–7

Italian excavations. *Year's Work in Classical Studies*: 101–16.

Un incisore antiquario del Seicento. — A. Note intorno alla vita ed opere di Giacomo Lauro. *Bibliofilia* 28: 361–73.

1927

*(with S. Walsh) Alessandro Specchi. *Town Planning Review* 12 (4): 237–48.

(with W. Dougill) The Capitol, Rome. Its history and development. *Town Planning Review* 12 (3): 159–80.

Il diritto del popolo di Roma sul Campidoglio e la donazione fatta da Carlo V ad Ascanio Caffarelli. *Capitolium* 3 (3): 132–5.

Un incisore antiquario del Seicento. — B. L'opera 'Antiquae Urbis Splendor'. *Bibliofilia* 29: 356–73.

Un mecenate inglese alla fine del settecento a Roma. *Roma* 5 (2): 52–62.

*Revision of and Introduction to *The Architecture of Ancient Rome* (*Architecture of Greece and Rome* (by W.J. Anderson and R.P. Spiers) 2). London, Batsford.

*The Roman Campagna in Classical Times. London, Benn. (Republished with an introduction by J.B. Ward-Perkins 1970 (London, Ernest Benn); Italian translation, *La campagna romana nell'età classica*, published 1982 (Milan, Longanesi).)

*La Via Tiburtina. *Atti e Memorie della Società Tiburtina di Storia e d'Arte* 7: 107–30.

1927–8

Italian excavations. *Year's Work in Classical Studies*: 115–28.

1928

La fine della Torre Cartularia. *Roma* 6 (3): 97–8.

Per la topografia storica della Campagna Romana. *Athenaeum. Studi Periodici di Letteratura e Storia dell'Antichità* 4: 7.

*Scrittori contemporanei di cose romane: Rodolfo Lanciani. *Archivio della Reale Società Romana di Storia Patria* 51: 103–43.

*La Via Tiburtina. *Atti e Memorie della Società Tiburtina di Storia e d'Arte* 8: 3–44.

(with G. Lugli) La villa dei Flavi cristiani "ad duas lauros" ed il suburbano imperiale ad oriente di Roma. *Memorie della Pontificia Accademia Romana di Archeologia* 2: 157–92.

1928–9

Italian excavations. *Year's Work in Classical Studies*: 119–30.

1929

Ancora S. Matteo in Merulana. *Roma* 7: 128.

Il castello d'acqua arcaico del Tuscolo. *Bullettino della Commissione Archeologica Comunale di Roma* 57: 161–82.

*Completion and revision of second edition of S.B. Platner, *A Topographical Dictionary of Ancient Rome*. London/Oxford, Oxford University Press.

Un incisore antiquario del Seicento. — C. L'heroico splendore della città del mondo. *Bibliofilia* 31: 105–22.

(with G.A. Butling) The Piazza di S. Ignazio, Rome: its history and development. *Town Planning Review* 13 (3): 139–48.

Recent criticism of Roman architecture. *Journal of the Royal Institute of British Architects* 37: 115–26.

La rete stradale romana nell'Etruria meridionale. *Studi Etruschi* 3: 171–85.

Rome. The Eternal City (Benn's Sixpenny Library 92). London, E. Benn.

Some Italian Scenes and Festivals. London, Methuen & Co. Ltd. (Italian revised edition — *Sagre e feste d'Abruzzo*, Ortona, 1995)

The Temple of Castor and Pollux in Rome. *Journal of Roman Studies* 19: 161–3.

1930

Italian excavations. *Year's Work in Classical Studies*: 115–24.

Recent discoveries in Italy. *Antiquaries Journal* 10: 258–63.

1931

The new piano regolatore for Rome. *Town Planning Review* 14 (4): 238–42.

(with A. Boethius) Le porte delle mure ciclopiche di Praeneste. *Bollettino dell'Associazione Internazionale di Studi Mediterranei* 2 (1): 17.

1932

(with G. Lugli) La basilica di Giunio Basso sull'Esquilino. *Rivista di Archeologia Cristiana* 9 (3–4): 221–55.

1935

The Aqueducts of Ancient Rome. Oxford, Clarendon Press. (Italian edition – *Gli acquedotti dell'antica Roma* (ed. G. Pisani Sartorio) (Rome, 1991).)

MAJOR WORKS ABOUT THOMAS ASHBY AND HIS COLLECTIONS

Archeologia a Roma nelle fotografie di Thomas Ashby 1891–1930. Milan, Electa, 1989.

Il Lazio di Thomas Ashby 1891–1930. Rome, Fratelli Palombi Editore, 1994.

Thomas Ashby. Un archeologo fotografa la Campagna Romana tra '800 e '900. Rome, De Luca Editore, 1986.

*Anderson, J.C. (1991) *Roman Brickstamps: The Thomas Ashby Collection in the American Academy at Rome (Archaeological Monographs of the British School at Rome* 3). London, British School at Rome.

*Bodart, D. (1975) *Dessins de la collection Thomas Ashby à Bibliothèque Vaticane (Biblioteca Apostolica Vaticana, Documenti e riproduzioni* 2). Vatican City, Biblioteca Apostolica Vaticana.

*Keaveney, R. (1988) *Views of Rome. From the Thomas Ashby Collection in the Vatican Library*. London, Scala Publications.

*Lugli, G. (1946) Piccole avventure romane di un archeologo militante. *Strenna di Romanisti* 7: 42–50.

*Tomassetti, F. (1927) Scrittori contemporanei di cose romane: Thomas Ashby. *Archivio della Reale Società Romana di Storia Patria* 50: 77–123.

INDEX

Related titles published by the British School at Rome

* ❖ *A Short History of the British School at Rome*
  by T.P. Wiseman (1990)

* ❖ *Lutyens in Italy: The Building of the British School at Rome*
  by Hugh Petter (1992)

* ❖ *Notes from Rome*
  by Rodolfo Lanciani, edited by Anthony Cubberley (1998)

* ❖ *Roman Brickstamps: The Thomas Ashby Collection in the American Academy at Rome*
  by J.C. Anderson (1991)

and by the same author:
* ❖ *San Vincenzo al Volturno 1: The 1980–86 Excavations Part I*
  edited by Richard Hodges (1993)

* ❖ *San Vincenzo al Volturno 2: The 1980–86 Excavations Part II*
  edited by Richard Hodges (1994)

For further information on all British School at Rome publications contact: The British School at Rome, at The British Academy, 10 Carlton House Terrace, London SW1Y 5AH.